CHASING CENTAURS

Around Pelion
in Greece

Catherine Ham

OneShoe Press

In memory of my Mother
Aspasia Calvocoressi

CONTENTS

CONTENTS CON'T.

INTRODUCTION

In the Long Ago, so long ago that even the greatest minds have not yet fully understood it, huge masses were hurled about. Water rose and sank as it found its way, and from this upheaval Mount Pelion was formed. Standing guard over Thessaly the mountain watched and made no comment as a civilization and a culture were shaped, as ancient battles were fought and myths were born.

My friend in London recommended Pelion to me. My husband and I came to this little-known part of Greece, summer playground of the Olympian gods, ancestral home of the fabled centaurs, and fell completely under its spell.

Frequently described as the Alps of Greece, Pelion's landscape is magnificent. Breathtaking scenery surrounded us every step of the way. Layers of antiquity awaited our discovery of this history, from mountain to sea. But it was the people of Pelion, shaped by generations of hard working, God-fearing folk, whose generosity of spirit enveloped us with warmth and kindness, who drew us back again and again.

PELION

GREECE

CONFUSED IN ATHENS

"Is this the right place?"

I looked around. We were waiting to collect our baggage but the luggage carousel, which showed weary signs of long and hard use, was motionless. "Maybe the bags are coming out somewhere else."

"It looks to be ... these people were all on the plane with us."

Fellow passengers were standing about in various states of impatience and indignation. Carry-on luggage, carelessly dumped onto the scarred floor, provided an irritating hazard to those pacing up and down.

Our pilot had made a textbook landing in Athens, and I'd been charmed when the Greek passengers aboard had clapped as we touched down. Considering I'd noticed several crossing themselves as we began our approach, I wasn't sure if these devout souls were applauding the pilot, or thanking the Almighty for delivering them safely.

It had been many long years since I'd last flown into Athens with my Mother, and I teared up as we passed over the Acropolis which she had held so closely in her heart.

The flights from Texas had been long but without incident. The landing had been on time. Yes, but time is a relative concept and so it was in the hubbub of the old Athens airport, the Hellinikon International Airport. Built in 1938 shortly before the Nazi invasion of 1941, it was captured and used by the Luftwaffe for the duration of the devastating occupation of Greece.

Today you fly into Eleftherios Venizelos, the attractively modern new international airport serving Athens.

Immigration had been a brief formality and we'd proceeded to the baggage claim where we armed ourselves with a luggage cart. And there we waited. And waited. And waited. We inquired and were answered with shrugs. We asked again. More shrugs. We trundled our carry on bags through the arrivals hall in search of answers. Nothing. We arranged ourselves on seats in the waiting area, and did just that. Waited. The knitting in my hand baggage saved my sanity. I shudder to think how I'd have coped if all my knitting projects had been in my missing luggage.

An hour passed during which no other flight arrived. Time seemed to have been put on hold. People fidgeted. Kiddies whined. Ron kept glancing at his watch. "I'd allowed five hours to drive from here to Pelion. I don't want to be driving at night. Not likely at this rate though. What's the problem? What the hell's going on?"

It was my turn to shrug.

At precisely 2:00 pm the luggage belt suddenly jolted into operation and porters miraculously appeared. Very odd. Wondering whether there was some kind of extended lunch break we weren't aware of, we grabbed our bags – which thankfully were among the first to be disgorged –

4

and made for Customs. To my great surprise we were through in a flash and headed towards the exit.

"Next stop's the car hire." Ron took the rental papers out of his pocket. "Over there."

We walked across to the offices housing the various firms and entered the relevant one, leaving our luggage outside the door. There was barely enough room for a couple of battered desks. Highly colored travel posters competed with tatty tapestries for the limited wall space. A rather overweight older man at one desk munched on some kind of pastry, while a much younger chap, shoulders slumped, stood staring through the glass front at the domestic arrivals concourse. The room was thick with cigarette smoke.

"Yes! Yes! Good afternoon," the seated man leapt up, sweeping the crumbs off the desk with his left hand while extending his right to Ron.

"Welcome! Welcome! We are so happy to see you."

He certainly seemed to be, his smile creasing his salt and pepper stubble. The sleeves of his faded blue shirt were roughly rolled up, his tie was loosely knotted halfway down his chest. Zorba. Anthony Quinn. He had a distinct look of Zorba. The younger man turned to face us. He was lean, smartly dressed, well groomed, and wearing a pair of very natty two-tone shoes. Were they about to break into a dance? I shook my tired head in an effort to clear it.

"How can we help you?"

Their English was good, with the charming accent many Greeks have when speaking English. It flashed through my mind that of course they would speak English for their business was almost certainly confined to foreign tourists. Ron and I weren't exactly draped with cameras but we hardly appeared to be locals.

Ron handed him the rental agreement, together with his passport, International Driving Permit and Texas driver's license.

"Ah! You are American," the older guy beamed at us. "Taki!" he turned to his assistant, "From Texas. *Americanos*. He is from Texas. A cowboy!"

Taki nodded.

"Dallas? The television. You know the Dallas?" His boss looked from Ron to me, his face wreathed in happy smiles. "I love the Dallas. I not miss one time to see the television for the Dallas. I love. Everybody love Dallas. Yes, the Dallas."

Taki, clearly unimpressed, continued to nod. "Yes, Nikos."

I felt for Taki. He was an infant when Dallas and the doings of the Ewings were gripping imaginations around the world. But Nikos wasn't to be stopped.

"You have been maybe to Dallas?" he asked of Ron. My heart sank. If Ron were to agree, I could see us being there for hours. And of course he did.

"Yes, oh yes. I lived there for thirteen years. My house was two miles from Southfork."

Nikos was electrified. "Taki! *Kafé*! At once! *Kyria*, lady, please to sit here." He pulled out an office chair which looked as exhausted as I felt. "We must drink a coffee after your long journey. Taki will go bring. Sit! Sit! Please."

I hesitated, torn. The hospitality of the Greeks is legendary. By the time I'd managed to find my voice, Taki was halfway out the door.

"You are very kind. Very, very kind. Thank you so much but we really cannot stay. We have a long way to drive and we must be going. We're really very sorry."

Such a look of disappointment on his face. The poor man. A long and boring day about to be enlivened by coffee with one who could talk with authority on Dallas, only to have his hopes dashed. We would certainly have enjoyed the interlude, but time was of the essence and we needed all the available daylight for our drive. In retrospect we should have accepted his kind offer, spent the night in an Athens hotel and continued the next day. But we didn't, and isn't hindsight a wonderful thing?

So it was that coffee was not taken. Papers were signed, handshakes exchanged and we followed Taki out to the parking lot to collect the car.

And a rather strange one it seemed to us, unfamiliar as America was in those days with Hyundai. Taki began extolling the virtues of the vehicle, a white Elantra, and frowned as Ron photographed the few scrapes it displayed. He didn't comment though and helped us stow the bags, pointed out the exit and politely left.

We adjusted the seats. I hung my camera around my neck and took two knitting projects out of my bag. Uninterrupted knitting time lay ahead. Ron handed me a map, together with the sheet of directions the leasing agent had provided.

"You'll be the navigator, Cathy. It looks pretty straightforward though. He seems to have laid it all out very clearly."

We settled in for the drive to the Pelion Peninsula, the starting point for our long-planned Greek vacation. Ron had recently completed a highly challenging engineering project for a client, and badly needed a rest. I'd been looking forward to a quiet exploration of a relatively unknown part of Greece described as magical, but a spanner, or should I say a knitting needle, had been thrown into the works. Shortly before we were due to leave, I found myself unexpectedly under contract to produce a knitting book within a very tight time frame. Not a problem in itself, but I needed to take many of the projects and all the required knitting yarns with me, and that of course meant a great deal of luggage.

"Ready?" Ron started the car. Ahead lay Pelion, home of the fabled centaurs, from where Jason and his Argonauts set out in search of the Golden Fleece.

❖ ❖ ❖

"This car handles very nicely," said Ron, as we drove out of the airport and onto the main road. "I'm quite impressed with it. We'll need to turn soon. At the Shell garage. It's on your side."

"OK, I'm looking."

"Are you sure you haven't seen it?"

We'd been driving for about twenty minutes.

"There should've been a Shell garage by now, according to this."

I'd not stopped staring at the motley collection of buildings alongside the road. "No, nothing. We've passed a BP garage and one called Avin, but I'm telling you there wasn't a Shell garage."

"Avin?" Ron swerved to avoid a suicidal motorcyclist whose crash helmet was swinging from the handlebars. "Never heard of it. It's a gas station, you say? Must be a Greek company."

I studied the page of directions we'd printed out from the agent's emails. "Yes, it definitely says to turn right at the Shell garage."

"Can you go over it again? I can't take my eyes off the road. These drivers are unbelievable – as bad as Cairo. Worse really."

Motorbikes, cars, trucks and heavy machinery jostled for position in a frenzy of movement and noise, horns blaring non stop, while nimble pedestrians wove through them in death-defying dance. A bug-eyed little boy, his nose pressed hard to the window, stared at me, unblinking, as we drove alongside his beat up family car. I

9

smiled at him. He stuck his tongue out at me. Perhaps he was also having a bad day.

"No, no, this can't be right, Cathy. There's something wrong here. I've followed his map to the letter, so where's the garage? We should have passed it long ago."

"Yes, something's not right."

"Look, we need to get out of Athens and then go north. That's what I'm going to do."

"I think we're somewhere around Glyfada … that sign says Glyfada."

"Well yes, the airport is in Glyfada, but we're moving away from Glyfada now. It's behind us. That sign's been knocked out of position."

We were to be in this wealthy suburb of Athens again one day, but we didn't know it then. Nor could we have known under what circumstances.

Ron, his eyes fixed on the road, tugged at the zipper pull on his jacket. "If you can, get this off and give it to me, then I can navigate."

He was referring to the keyring compass I'd bought him years ago. He still loves to bug me with it. We'll be on a plane and he'll point it at the cockpit and say: "The pilot's doing OK. We're heading in the right direction."

Mind you, prior to the widespread use of GPS that little compass got us out of several wrong turns. Good ole' L.L. Bean!

We had to stop at the next traffic light, giving Ron a chance to orient himself. "The E75 is the highway that goes north to Volos, so keep your eyes peeled for a road sign. We're heading towards Athens now … we'll pick up the highway there."

I was checking my knitting when a cacophony of car horns alerted us to the change in the traffic lights. We drove on. Had we not, we might well have been mown down. We learnt very quickly that there's really just one rule of the road in Greece: there are no rules of the road. At least that's the belief of many of the drivers.

❖ ❖ ❖

The traffic congestion in Athens is so bad that road rationing is in place at specific periods of the year. This is a complicated system of license plate numbers, days of the month and days of the week. Plates ending in odd numbers may only be on the road if the dates end in odd numbers, and ditto for even numbers. Thus if your license number ends in 1,3,5,7,9 you may drive in certain designated parts of downtown Athens on odd-numbered days, and so on. And if that strikes you as convoluted, factor in that this arrangement does not apply on weekends and official holidays. The rule is relaxed when the public transport unions call a strike, which is not infrequent. You're probably thinking that chaos is bound to ensue, but somehow the traffic manages to muddle along.

"Normally I could navigate by the sun, but obviously not now, Cathy."

Intermittent cloud cover had started to obscure the sun, and being unfamiliar then with Greek weather patterns I couldn't judge the outcome. Rain? A storm? Would it blow over? Now I'm well aware of the whims and wiles of the weather gods. I know how fickle they can be, how temperamental. We've witnessed the ferocious marital spats of Zeus and Hera up there on Mt. Olympus and have learnt to pay attention when they start to argue. I suppose you could say we eavesdrop, but we can't always be sure which direction their row will take.

Signs indicating Piraeus, the port city of Athens, had begun to appear.

"I think we're going too far," said Ron. "No, we've definitely gone too far. We should have turned through the downtown area already … I'll have to backtrack."

Easier said than done. The map we'd been sent was next to useless. We discovered later that it was outdated, and that the Shell garage had been demolished some time ago. No wonder we were thoroughly confused. The business owner, most of whose clients would have come to Pelion via Athens, had neglected to stay informed of any changes in the area.

The fevered flow of traffic made it extremely difficult to move fast enough across the lanes to access an exit, and whenever we managed to we invariably encountered a no-entry sign or, as in one hair-raising moment, a donkey cart. The donkey was unfazed though we were somewhat shaken as we swung back into the main stream of vehicles. It hardly seemed possible that the traffic could get any thicker, but we were approaching a major port of international significance and every form of vehicular transport appeared hellbent on reaching it. Haulage juggernauts laden with shipping containers, tankers, garbage trucks, buses, taxis, cars, motorbikes and scooters stampeded down the road, while bicycles and even adult tricycles swayed along the edges, many of them piled perilously high with goods.

The fumes and billowing smoke seeped through the various shapes and sizes of the traffic, giving the appearance of a raging torrent seething its way down to the sea. This logjam resembled the assorted debris that smashes down in floodwaters, with the heavier items crushing the smaller items struggling not to become submerged. The clamor was deafening. I reflected on the contrast between present day and prehistoric times. Founded in the 5th century BC, Piraeus has an extremely long and distinguished history. There are archaeological sites of great significance, several museums and many sporting venues in the area. We needed to get away from it as quickly as possible.

"Brace yourself, Cathy." We were stopped at the front of traffic for a light. As soon as the signal turned green Ron shot forward like a racehorse at the starting gates, making a sharp right turn into the relative calm of a smaller side street. "Phew! That was close. I wasn't sure if the car had the acceleration. OK, back into town we go."

All credit to Ron who steered our nerve-wracking way through the bedlam of the Athens traffic, where traffic regulations weren't much observed by the motorists. To this pandemonium add the unfamiliar city, and the whole exercise became exceedingly stressful.

At one point the sun made a brief appearance to our left.

"Good, I'm correct. We're moving north like I wanted."

I felt myself relax a little, though I kept my eyes fixed on the road signs for the E75, part of the International E-road network of Europe. Before long we were traveling on it through the northern suburbs, away from Athens towards the port city of Volos, and from there down the Pelion Peninsula to the holiday house we'd rented in Kalamos.

ALL THE WAY TO KALAMOS

At that time the road hugged the coastline for a large part of the journey. You drove through each of the villages that laze along the sea, taking your time to stop for a coffee or a pleasantly relaxed lunch at the waterside. Traditional wooden *caïques* whose design dates back millennia to the time of Homer, bob about with other craft at their moorings just a few yards away. Today there is a new highway, built with EU money. It has many of the advantages that such highways do, though now it's almost clinically efficient in comparison to the old road. The tunnels cut deep into the mountains and while they slash the traveling time, they make me feel detached from the people, the sea and landscape. Most of the coastal villages are bypassed but can still be reached from the new road. Drivers with a need for speed probably prefer this new route. I certainly don't.

"Well, there we are … look at that," I pointed to a sign up ahead. "A Shell garage. Finally. What a joke!"

"I think I'll pull in … I don't trust the fuel gauges on rental cars. Can't hurt to fill up."

"Good. I've got to pee. Badly. And we can buy a bottle of water."

While Ron and the assistant dealt with the car, I went inside in search of the toilet. The woman behind the counter smiled and pointed to the door marked WC. I expect she was accustomed to travelers. Pushing open the door, I closed it behind me, turned, and stared. On the floor or should I rather say, set into the floor, was a white porcelain affair. It took a few seconds for it to dawn on me that this was it. This was the toilet. I admit I was horrified. I shouldn't have been for it was spotlessly clean, but it certainly was not like any toilet I had ever used. Yes, I'd seen them. Very briefly. Hadn't paid much attention to them. Major airports have both kinds for the convenience of passengers from the East and from the West. These are often referred to as Turkish toilets, or squat toilets. I'm not going to go into the specifics of how one uses such a commode. Yes, I fully appreciate that they have a long history, and no, I'm not about to write a paper on toilets.

A chain hung down at the back of it. Glancing up I saw that it was connected to a water tank, and that much higher up the wall, almost at ceiling height, was a small window with a rope attached to it. Hemingway flashed into my mind – the accident he'd had in his apartment in Paris, when he'd split his head by pulling the cord for the skylight instead of the one to flush the toilet. A very serious accident indeed, with lifelong repercussions for him. I didn't linger a moment longer.

"All right?" Ron looked at me as I emerged.

"Let's just go."

We drove away. I explained my predicament to Ron. "Look, I'd rather we find a bush at the side of the road. I'll manage, but there's no way I'm using that."

He was most sympathetic. "There'll be one somewhere soon. Don't worry. Can you hang on a while?"

We came upon a small cafe a short time later where the toilet was familiar. Upstanding. I was much relieved.

❖ ❖ ❖

The sun burst out of hiding as we neared Thermopylae. It seemed appropriate that it should shine upon a site we'd both dreamed of seeing since childhood. My Mother had often told me the tale of the Greeks and Persians at the battle there, but I was young then and only began to appreciate the pride and longing in her voice when I was older. Ron drove as slowly as he could past the monument to Leonidas and his tiny band of heroes, but we couldn't spare the daylight driving time to stop. We did manage a look at the surrounding area, trying to pinpoint the mountain pass where Leonidas, king of Sparta, and his men died defending their country against the might of the invading Persians.

Ron explained how the topography has changed over the many centuries. "The actual battlefield is now under all the soil chucked out from the hot springs and the river, and the alluvial soil washed down from the mountain. That's been flooding forever, and more and more soil and rock has been heaped all over the place. The coastline will also have moved out because of earthquakes and storms. I think the pass is still there – not likely to have changed much at all. We'll stop when we return to Athens."

That we did, and I was then to have my own bit of drama.

❖ ❖ ❖

The drive began to seem endless, though it wasn't punctuated by cries of: "Are we there yet?"

Signs indicating Volos came into view and soon Volos itself, spreading out ahead of us in a great sprawl sandwiched between Mt. Pelion, home of the mythical centaurs, and the Pagasitic Gulf. Here on the mountain's forested slopes the Olympic gods spent their summers, invisible to the mortals but occupying the same world. These living arrangements would have suited Zeus very well for he could pursue fair maidens with wild abandon through the lovely glades. His wife, Hera? Not so thrilled.

As if in welcome, the last of the clouds disappeared behind the fabled mountain. On its slopes Chiron, the most famous of the centaurs, taught many of the heroes of Greek mythology, including Jason who gathered his Argonauts and sailed away to find the Golden Fleece, and Achilles, the greatest warrior of all.

We drove into Volos, which was slowly coming back to life after the afternoon break, and out onto the road that winds down the Pelion

Peninsula. The harbor lies behind you at this point and it's easy to see why it's been so vital to maritime activity for thousands of years. We knew little of the history of Volos then and even less of Thessaly, but as it turned out we were going to learn more. Much more.

Words do not do justice to the beauty of the Pagasitic Gulf. When the waters are calm, when you fancy you can feel the breath of a butterfly, the Aegean masquerades as seams of lapis and turquoise under the protection of glass. When the Greek gods are angered and storms thrash its waters the Aegean rages in retaliation, hurling furious waves at all in its path, flinging itself in tantrums at the shoreline, foaming incoherently in its displeasure. All was tranquil on the water that late afternoon however, and the traffic minimal. To say we were exhausted is an understatement, but with the Pagasitic to our right and Mt. Pelion rising to its heights on our left, we began to thrill with anticipation.

On and on Ron drove. The sun made its languid way down towards the far horizon, streaking sea and sky in red and gold. I fancied it was regretting its hide-and-seek behavior of earlier. An exhausted Ron gave all his attention to the unfamiliar road, twisting and turning through villages and farmland while I, free of such concentration, knitted and dozed, dozed and knitted.

◆ ◆ ◆

We passed through Argalasti, gateway to the stunning villages of the South Pelion, and started down the winding road to Kalamos. That first sight from high above the sea, with Mt. Pelion standing watch over the Gulf, and the sun glinting on the brilliant blue water as it began thinking of taking its rest in the west, will remain with me forever.

In those days the road to Kalamos consisted of dirt and gravel, with a good serving of ruts and great dollops of rocks. It wound through olive groves and past old stone houses. It meandered down almost to the water's edge and then took a sharp right turn between a small beach on one side and a few buildings on the other. Following the directions sent to us we continued along the narrow road, literally a few yards from the water. Turning right again we drove across the bridge – just barely wide enough to allow a small car – and over the dry river to the other side. The dirt track bounced along onto a tiny concrete strip fronting the water. I wonder how many tourists have found themselves unexpectedly immersed in the Pagasitic there?

"That must be the house," Ron pointed to a whitewashed cottage at the far end of the small beach. "It shows it on these directions. Magda's house. He tells us here where to find the key."

We parked the Elantra parallel to the water, alarmingly close to it, but there was nowhere else to leave it. I climbed out, seized a bag and began to totter along the sand, my legs protesting after the many hours we'd spent seated.

Hearing voices, I glanced at the corner building. It seemed to be a little *taverna* of sorts, with some women seated on a bench under a great mulberry tree. Their conversation stopped. We nodded at them as they stared at us trudging back and forth from the car to the cottage with the bags. Lots of bags, for I had many items to knit for the looming book deadline. Ron had opened the gate into a courtyard with a large table on which we began placing the bags.

The ladies resumed their conversation.

"They're English, obviously …"

"No, they look like Germans …"

"What are you talking about? They're speaking English …"

"But they're a lot older than the people who come to Magda's house…"

"It's past the high season now … those who come in summer are kids …"

"Yes, and they do nothing but drink beer and party all night …"

"I don't think these will be noisy …"

"Look at all the bags – why so many …?"

"You think maybe others are still coming …?"

"I'll ask Magda …"

"Pah, she won't know, she only knows to have the house ready …"

Ron locked the car and we walked past the little group for the last time that evening.

I smiled at them and spoke: "*Kali nichta sas, kyries.*" The deafening silence followed us back to Magda's house. "Good night, ladies."

MAGDA'S HOUSE

The sun was sinking very fast into the sea as we dumped the last of the bags down on the terrace table.

"Right, I'll get the key." Ron retrieved it from the spot the agent had indicated, and unlocked the door. We stepped inside. My immediate impression was one of size. Small and snug, that entrance room was clearly the kitchen but I was so tired that few details registered.

The journey had been long and not without stress. Night had fallen. A bath and a bed were all I could think of. The bathroom itself was surprisingly large, somewhat bigger than the kitchen, but devoid of a bathtub. No long soak for the aching body then.

"What happened to the bath? Ron, where's the bath?" Fastened to the wall was the type of handheld shower that one commonly finds as part of the fixtures of a modern bathtub. That really useful item for hosing off your feet, the kids and the dog.

"Doesn't look like there was ever a tub here, Cathy. I think this is meant to be the shower."

It was, and like so many other tourists in Greece at that time we were about to make our acquaintance with it. Take a look at some of the travel reviews on the web and you'll see what I mean. Greek bathrooms are often quite small though perfectly functional, and while more modern homes will probably have bathtubs, rental properties aren't always equipped with them. Water. That's the reason. Water.

Having grown up in South Africa I'm acquainted with water shortages, but these are occasioned by periodic drought. Greece is not a well-watered country, although it's better off in that regard than several of the Arab countries where Ron has spent much time. Hence the handheld shower. It saves water, for unless one is particularly agile or blessed with many arms like a Asian goddess, it's not that easy to hop about clutching at soap and hose and washcloth. The idea is to get yourself wet, turn off the water, lather up, and then retrieve the hose to rinse. In theory. Unfortunately many a water tank has been emptied because the great unwashed have allowed the hose to run while performing their ablutions.

The absent bathtub wasn't the only surprise. A note taped to the toilet tank, handwritten in English, proclaimed: "Use the bucket." A plastic bucket sat on the closed toilet seat. I stared at Ron.

"Use the bucket! What is this! We've paid all this money so we can go camping?"

"Don't worry," Ron soothed, "I'll work something out. The bucket simply means that the tank isn't filling from the water supply for some reason."

Using the shower hose, Ron filled the bucket and placed it next to the loo. "Here you go. I'll fill the tank each time we need it. This will take care of it for now, then we can talk to the agent and find out what's going on. At least it's not a long drop."

◆ ◆ ◆

We woke early the following morning, just after the sun had put in its appearance. In contrast to its cheerful beaming down upon our little courtyard, we stumbled groggily about. No human sound could be heard, only the soothing swish of the water and the humming of contented bees. A small welcome basket had greeted us on arrival with wine, fruit, olive oil, bread and some tea bags, and most welcome indeed were these provisions.

"I never thought I could drink tea without milk," I whined, "but thank goodness he left us this."

"Yes, saved our lives. But we need to find out what's going on with the toilet." Ron read through the agent's emails. "Look, here's the address."

Smartphones? Not yet in existence.

"His office is further down the coast, so let's get sorted out as soon as we can and go find him and some food."

The buzzing of the bees was getting louder. The droning became more and more insistent.

"They sound rather like a lawn mower, don't you think? They're not swarming, are they?"

As I uttered the words a small boat appeared on the left with two people in it, and made a sharp turn, cutting the engine a few yards in front of us. We stared as the occupants jumped out to pull it up onto the beach.

"Hello! Good morning!" a very English voice called to us, its owner walking across the sand to introduce himself as the agent we'd been dealing with.

"I'm really sorry about the toilet," he began by way of explanation. It seemed that the problem had been discovered the previous day when final preparations for our arrival were being made.

"It was too late for Magda to get hold of a plumber," he continued, "but I've brought him, and I don't think it's a big job."

It evidently wasn't for it was fixed in no time, and the two of them left the way they had come, flushed with success.

With sanitation restored and no immediate need to drive anywhere we settled back to contemplate our first full day together in Greece. And why the Pelion Peninsula? A good friend of mine, a South African living in London, had shared her hideaway with us. Not yet well known then, Pelion was a closely kept secret among a few lucky foreigners, and a great favorite of the Greeks themselves.

❖ ❖ ❖

Magda's house was - how should I put it? Basic. That pretty much covers it. There weren't any pictures of the interior on the agent's website when we'd booked, but there wasn't really any need for them. We'd asked for a place close to the water, and we certainly got it. Right at the furthest end of the village, tucked in the elbow of the headland that shelters Kalamos on the Pagasitic Gulf, the house was less than fifteen feet from the water.

It was spotlessly clean, with tiled stone floors and whitewashed walls.

"What are these tiles? They're rather unusual – all these small bits of color."

"Polished aggregate," replied Ron. "Various types of stone are crushed and then mixed with cement. The mixture can be used to cover large areas or is made into tiles. Then the surface is polished smooth."

"Well, one thing Greece isn't short of is rock, that's for sure."

"We had them in our house in Taiwan, when I was a kid," Ron was referring to his time there as a military brat during a crisis with the People's Republic of China, "but I also saw them quite often in mainland China on business years later."

The kitchen had a fireplace, as did all the rooms. There were several beds in these and I could understand why it appealed to young people who apparently came in large groups in the summer, but the plain wooden beds were served by rather awful mattresses. They were so lumpy that we suspected they were stuffed with horsehair, dating, as Ron put it, from the time of Alexander.

The little house was rich with warmth and sincerity. It struck me at the time that it was very simply furnished, but on reflection what did it really require except for the essentials? It was a beach cottage, after all, and as such more than adequate for those seeking sea and sun and for some, solitude. Magda had taken great care to decorate her home with the wealth of talent and skill in her hands, and the treasury of knowledge inherited from the womenfolk of her family. She had made the plastic armchairs very comfortable with plump, finely embroidered cushions, and had scattered bright rag rugs throughout the rooms. Each bed sported a colorful patchwork blanket. We certainly had no need of the blankets, but I appreciated their expert workmanship and the cozy welcome they provided.

Knowing they'd not be used in summer, Magda had screened the fireplaces with crocheted panels, and arranged beautifully worked covers in complex counted thread designs on the mantelpieces, all trimmed with her handmade lace. Intricately crocheted curtain panels hung at every window pane, depicting scenes abundant with baskets of flowers, foliage and gazelles. These were striking not only in the detailed motifs worked painstakingly into them, but also in the fact that no pattern was repeated anywhere throughout the rooms. It's probably fair to say that maybe not all guests in Magda's waterside home took much notice of the textiles, but I was filled with admiration for the quiet artistry displayed.

Unsophisticated Magda's house might have been, but oh the location! I doubt that even the most jaded world traveler could have found fault with it. The Peninsula tumbles down from the mountain as though making a determined bid for escape, rising and falling in rumpled folds to end in the sea, a short boat ride across from the island of Trikeri. And for all its frenzied flight when earth and sea were at the mercy of primordial forces, it came to rest facing the mountain from which it had sprung. The mountains on the far mainland, separated from the Peninsula by the Gulf, seem to be sliding down into the water, holding onto secrets they have no inclination to reveal.

A large rustic table sat outside in the small concrete courtyard, shaded by a tree of considerable age and size, and together with those ubiquitous white molded plastic chairs and recliners it was all we needed. From your seat at the handmade table you could see small fish darting about, and hold your breath as the gulls swooped at them. Three or four traditional boats, *caïques* swayed on the water, their reflected colors scattering rainbows shot with sunlight.

Built of stone, entirely by hand in the mid 1800s, at a time when there was no such thing as electricity nor any piped water from a regular source, Magda's house was a sturdy one. Houses like this would usually be occupied only in summer and during the olive harvest, for the heavy winter seas hurl rocks and driftwood high onto the narrow beaches and into the courtyards of the houses edging them. Flooding frequently occurs. The result is a frenzy of painting and repairing when spring begins to put an end to the bad weather.

The cottage had been much updated in that electricity had been installed, though somewhat haphazardly, and the bathroom was probably a storeroom prior to its conversion. Rough and ready though it was, it provided the necessary indoor plumbing to make the property acceptable as a holiday let. For the elderly widowed Magda the income was a godsend.

❖ ❖ ❖

The little house was the stuff of picture postcards with its blue-painted windows, shutters and doors. The stone walls were draped in great swathes of bougainvillea which leapt at every opportunity onto the olive trees and across the tiled roof, competing for attention with the cheerful tubs of geraniums grouped about in colorful profusion. Picturesque, we would call it. Charming. Was Magda's life there as a young bride a charmed one? Not by our standards. Not at all. Springs in the area provided fresh water, but it had to be carried to the point of use. Those romantic paintings one sees in museums and on postcards, of peasant women in traditional dress bearing heavy jars of water, belie the harsh reality of this body-breaking toil. Every drop is precious. Throughout the centuries and throughout the civilizations people and donkeys have labored steadily at this and other heavy tasks. Their very survival depended upon it. Firewood had to be collected, carried and chopped for cooking and for heat. Game had to be hunted, and domestic animals cared for. Food was organic, yes, but it was backbreaking work that produced it.

The classic Mediterranean diet, consisting of the foodstuffs endorsed nowadays as vital to good health, was not so much a considered choice as it was a necessary one. I don't for a moment question its obvious benefits, but I often find myself reflecting on the role of stress. Our lives, if not our arteries, are clogged with tension and anxiety. Can that be offset by a perfect diet? I'm not sure. That typical diet was dependent on both the environment and the seasons. In addition, Greece has suffered many an invasion and many a disaster of climate over the centuries, meaning that food wasn't always abundantly available.

TEA FOR TWO

Ron and I needed to eat. Our hearts and minds might have been absorbed with wonder at our surroundings, our stomachs however were demanding. In spite of the provisions in the welcome basket, we hadn't actually had a proper meal for many hours, and were in desperate need of coffee and more tea. We set off to search for some, but we didn't have to go far.

We left Magda's courtyard and trod along the sand, shells, stones and various bits of detritus that edged the water. Two people were drinking coffee outside on the small promenade in front of the cafe we'd passed the previous night. They watched us with interest as we approached, and became quite animated when I greeted them in Greek. Coffee was immediately offered and gratefully accepted. Mr and Mrs Bakaloni, or Bakaloni and *kyria* Katina as we were soon to call them, were the owners of the two-storey building.

We chatted a while. *Kyria* Katina was interested in my knitting, and examined it carefully.

"But it's still summer. Why are you working on a jacket now? The winter is still a long way off."

I explained to her about the knitting book and the extremely limited time I had to complete it in. She was a little puzzled.

"But you are on holiday. You shouldn't be carrying knitting about with you. You are here to rest, to enjoy yourself."

"Yes, but I knit all the time anyway, *kyria* Katina. I love to knit. It's very relaxing for me. I enjoy creating new designs. The book isn't a problem, but time is."

She seemed unconvinced, and I could see her point. Sitting a few feet from the water, drinking in the sweetest of air along with the delicious coffee, it required something of an effort to remind myself of life at a more hectic pace.

The Bakaloni establishment wasn't a taverna, but more of a coffee shop. Called a *kaffenion* in Greek, such a place is licensed to sell coffee and alcoholic drinks, *ouzo* being typical. Various appetizers, known as *meze* will be served with the ouzo. One can make quite a repast from the meze, but the complete meals one finds in restaurants aren't sold. Of course, the more ouzo one drinks, and the more friends one's drinking with, the greater the variety and quantity of the morsels which are brought to one's table.

They described the pattern of their summers. Renting rooms to holiday makers, serving coffees and drinks, together with selling bread, milk and a small selection of essential commodities was how they made their living. Short, wiry, and as active as any grasshopper, Bakaloni, we would later find out, was a retired policeman. Comfortably plump and very pleasant, and seeming to be of a more placid disposition, *kyria* Katina helped in every capacity. The attractive frock she was wearing had immediately caught my eye for although the fabric was printed, the patterning on it was in the style of handwoven ikat cloth, for which I have great admiration.

Situated at the very edge of the water, with a tiny jetty where boats could tie up and one step would place you right among the inviting tables covered in cheery oilcloths, Bakaloni's place was well patronized. And it certainly helped to have one of the very few telephones in the area. Some sort of system metered the length and cost of a call, and apart from being most convenient in those early and very expensive days of mobile phones, it brought regular custom to their business.

In the exhaustion and confusion of the previous evening we'd failed to notice the few shelves of items for sale inside. It was in effect the tiniest of shops, but oh joy, I spotted a box of Lipton's tea. One hundred Lipton tea bags in the bright yellow box! I like my tea strong. It has to kick start my morning, with constant doses throughout the day lest I should begin to flag. To achieve this in the absence of my preferred brand of tea, I take two Lipton's bags per mug. This box, waiting for me on the middle shelf, was just the ticket to keep me going until we could find a grocery store.

"I'll have the box of tea, please," I said to Bakaloni as Ron checked out the rather meager supply of dairy products in the chiller. In all fairness, it was the end of the season and the little enterprise would soon close down for the winter, whereupon the elderly couple would return to Argalasti to spend the winter.

Bakaloni took the box from the shelf. "How many do you want?"

"Oh, I only need one," I replied.

He reached into the box, which I then noticed was already opened, took out one teabag in its little packet and laid it on the counter.

I stared, confused. "No, I want the whole box," I finally managed to say.

"The whole box!" he exclaimed. "You can't have the whole box. I don't sell the whole box." He placed two more teabags on the counter. "Isn't that enough?"

Who was he kidding? "No, I need more. Lots more," I stretched my hand out for the box. He quickly pulled it away from me, and added one more teabag to the pile.

It was evident that we could play tea for two all day at that rate.

"Ten! I want at least ten. Don't you want to sell them? Why won't you sell them to me?"

"Six, no more. Six. You can have six," countered Bakaloni, putting the box back on the shelf.

"What does it matter if I buy all of them? You want to sell them, don't you?" But I knew by his expression that he had won. Ron calls this little exchange the Kalamos tea party but it wasn't funny at the time.

With me clutching my teabags and Ron carrying the rest of our provisions we walked back to Magda's. Using the crockery provided, we laid bread, butter, milk, cheese, some cold meat, the one slightly battered tomato Bakaloni had left, together with grapes and apples out on the courtyard table, put the kettle to boil on the gas cooking plate in the kitchen, and were set for a late lunch.

◆ ◆ ◆

It would be easy to wax lyrical about the simple enjoyment of the meal. To take flights of fancy with descriptions of birdsong accompanied by the gentle murmuring of the water telling and retelling its ancient tales, but somehow that would be to detract from the uncomplicated pleasure of the moment. We ate our fill and settled back in our chairs.

Ron dozed a bit. Hardly surprising after all the stress of the trip and the long drive, but I knitted away steadily, the book deadline ever threatening, though I was able to relieve some of the pressure by eating almost all of the chocolate we had bought from Bakaloni. The sea barely rippled. All was still, drowsy, but suddenly the no longer sleepy water surged forward several feet, right up to the table. Startled, we looked out to sea.

"That's really odd," said Ron. "I don't see any boat out there that could have set up such a wake."

We made more tea. That took care of the remaining teabags, and we drank it while discussing our options for the evening meal. A drive to Argalasti, the upper village, was decided upon for there are butchers and tiny shops selling a variety of groceries and we needed to get supplies.

We had left the Hyundai to the side of Bakaloni's building – there was no other place to park it – but when we began to climb in a woman bustled out of the adjoining house to make her feelings clear.

"You can't leave it here," she announced, hand on hip. "You are not allowed to park here."

That was debatable for there was no sign indicating this, nor was the car obstructing anything. No point in arguing for she was obviously of the type who object to practically everything. We did notice however that her paying guests used the same spot.

The narrow road up to Argalasti bumped and snaked its unpaved way past the old stone houses in those days, cutting through olive groves and across rock-strewn fields, finally reaching the tarred road. I was knitting all the way.

We parked in front of the church and headed to the bakery. There was a TV fastened to the wall, with a small knot of people staring at it. The screen was filled with scenes of police and emergency vehicles, frantic people being interviewed.

"What's happened?" I asked. "What's happened?"

"*Seismos*! Athena!" came the reply. "Athens! There's been a big earthquake!"

❖ ❖ ❖

I was stunned. I'd had no experience of earthquake, but Ron had. Earthquakes to me were disasters that happened in distant lands, to people I had little connection with. TV news would cover the events from every angle, sometimes for several days, but I was always detached from it. This was different. The part of Athens affected was the northern suburbs we'd so very recently driven through.

"It looks bad," Ron said as we continued to gaze at the TV, jostling for space as more and more people came in to watch. Ron has been through tremors and large '
quakes in many countries, and was directly involved with relief efforts in the aftermath of the Good Friday earthquake in Alaska. The images on the screen were distressing, and perhaps even more so because I could understand what was being said. The horror, the shock, the grief were almost palpable.

We left the bakery and went into the little supermarket next door. We barely spoke as we selected a few groceries, not even commenting when we put an unopened box of Lipton's teabags into the basket. We paid and returned to the car.

"I suppose we'd better find a butcher," said Ron, looking around. We walked up the slope from the church, and soon came across one. The butcher got up from his chair behind the counter to greet us, keeping one eye on the TV set high on the wall above racks of sausage. I don't recall what was said. I have no recollection of what we bought. I can still see the devastation being broadcast on the TV. We met Yianni that dreadful day, and he's been our butcher ever since.

◆ ◆ ◆

We'd planned on having a meal in one of the local tavernas but somehow it didn't seem appropriate to do so amidst all the distress, so we made our way back to Magda's, taking care not to be confronted again by She-Of-The-No-Parking. We could have challenged her on the parking rights but were reluctant to do so. What would the point have been? We were the outsiders after all. Just as well we didn't argue with her for now, living in close proximity to her as we do, it might well have made social relations difficult.

So we parked in a spot not likely to enrage her, though I'm not sure she'd even noticed us. She was sitting in silence with several others in front of Bakaloni's, listening to the steady stream of news coverage. After exchanging quiet greetings we made our way back to Magda's. To have begun any conversation felt like an intrusion. Ron, ever prepared, had packed a shortwave radio in our luggage; once he had tuned it, I was able to translate the reports for him.

It was grim. One hundred and forty three people had died. The damage to buildings was enormous and the financial losses proportionately large, but no amount of money can ever be equated to the loss of life. Earthquake is no stranger to Greece. She coexists with the threat just as San Francisco does. Life goes on.

"Remind me to get more batteries for the radio, Cathy, we'll need them," said Ron as he tended the chops on the small charcoal grill provided at Magda's house.

The air was still, the sea hardly whispered. Nature appeared silenced in respect. Ron turned off the radio. We began to eat, not speaking, so that even the noise of chewing seemed deafening. The occasional bat swooped without sound on a mosquito, and we lost ourselves in our thoughts.

TAVERNA GALINI

Sunshine, birds, and the lightest of breezes greeted our awakening. Far from the scene of the earthquake, the grief and the chaos, we prepared a simple breakfast. My thoughts kept wandering to those who were being rescued, to those who were risking their own lives searching all night among the rubble, and to those for whom rescue wasn't possible. The sea slipped back and forth onto the sand, while I worked the soothing stitches on my needles.

Ron brought me a fresh mug of tea. "Cathy, there really is nothing we can do to help, and it's a nice day. Let's go for a walk and look around a bit … we should get some exercise … jetlag's going to hit us soon."

I nodded and we set about tidying up. Nudged into a better frame of mind, we prepared to explore our surroundings, me with knitting in my hands and a camera in my pocket, Ron with whatever else I thought I'd need in his backpack. As usual I had extra knitting supplies.

The walk along the waterfront to the other side of Kalamos is literally at the water's edge and is not difficult, provided one has the ability to step with great care among the plastic bottles and beer cans wedged against the rocks, and the broken bits of walls that might have been parts of quays in years gone by. Maybe even buildings of some sort. Many years gone by, I reckon. But if the water gets a little agitated then it becomes more challenging to dart one's way through without getting wet. Getting wet doesn't bother me, but on this day all was still. This is the short way. The other way follows the track the car took to reach Bakaloni's, crossing the river by way of a small bridge and is not only longer, but winds well away from the water.

Most of the houses were shuttered up tightly and few people were about for the season was essentially over. We were to learn later that, as one person put it, the lights are switched off at the end of August. This was in the days before the arrival of the package holiday began to impact Pelion, when accommodations for tourists were mostly very simple, and only a handful of places offering meals could be found.

"Look," Ron pointed at a hand-painted wooden board, "somewhere to eat."

So it was. "Taverna Galini" proclaimed the lopsided sign on a gate that had clearly given up any effort to secure the entryway. We stepped through onto a swept concrete patio dotted with metal tables wearing checked cloths. Assorted chairs, some plastic and some rather rickety wooden ones with rush seats, waited patiently for customers as did the cats lounging under them.

We could hear a male voice reporting on the earthquake but couldn't tell if it came from radio or television. The place appeared deserted, not surprisingly for it was still early in the day, but within seconds a rather rotund man came bustling out from the building at the opposite end of the patio, a huge smile on his face. And so we met Vageli Michalis, habitually clad in a sleeveless cotton undershirt in summer, very seldom if ever to be seen with his teeth in his mouth, and owner, with his wife Eleftheria, of the establishment.

"Yes! Yes! Please?" he beamed, in heavily-accented English, for his practiced eye must have summed us up immediately. He was most gratified when I inquired in Greek if we might have a coffee.

"Please, please, sit down," he pulled out chairs for us and turned back into the building. We looked around. Each table sported a little jar of flowers. Tubs of ferns, thickly planted in painted oil cans were gathered up along the walls. Vageli returned with bottles of water, soon to be followed by Eleftheria, his wife, bearing a tray of coffees and drinking glasses. Vageli made the introductions, while Eleftheria served us. She was softly spoken and warmly welcoming, her graying black hair pulled back from her thin face. They both settled down to satisfy their curiosity about us.

Once they'd established where we were staying, the talk turned immediately to the earthquake. They were shocked by it, and greatly concerned.

"We're used to earthquake here. It's nothing new, but every time it's most upsetting," said Vageli.

Eleftheria nodded, her gnarled hands twisting and untwisting her apron. "You don't know if there will be more. You don't know what's going to happen next."

I translated quickly for Ron, who replied: "Please ask if they have family in Athens?"

"It appears they do have people in Athens," I explained to him, "but nobody of theirs is affected as far as they've heard."

Our conversation continued on the path that conversations typically take when people meet for the first time in relaxed circumstances. We learnt that the rather nondescript building was larger than it appeared from the pathway in front. It housed apartments available for rent, and a small shop carrying various odds and ends. Many of the holiday rentals in the area are self-catering, and Vageli's shop provided the basics a tourist might require. Plastic shoes hung from the ceiling, together with inflatable beach toys, fishing rods and umbrellas. Shelves held everything from aspirin and mosquito repellent, to shampoo, soap and deodorant; bread and cookies were contained in a basket on the counter, and cigarettes behind it; glass-fronted refrigerators worked through the summer heat to keep drinks, yoghurt and chocolate bars cool, while a mostly empty freezer housed a couple of ice creams left over from the summer rush, bits of bait and a plastic bag of small fish.

Tucked into every nook and cranny were sunhats and fishing nets, buckets and spades, beach towels, footballs, coloring books and a few magazines. Displays of sweets tempted from every angle. We were often to see swim-suited kiddies pondering their choices while adults debated the merits of various provisions.

Situated as it was at the opposite end of Kalamos from Bakaloni's, it tended not to offer much competition. The shop was a lifeline for the migrant workers who otherwise would need to walk about seven kilometers through rough terrain to Argalasti for goods. The plentiful supplies of chocolate weren't lost on me – I was relieved to note that tiny Kalamos had backup should Bakaloni be found wanting.

Vageli and Eleftheria would have talked all day and we would have been happy to listen, but we were eager to investigate the surroundings so after buying bottles of water, some sesame seed cookies and chocolate, we promised to come back that evening for dinner and took our leave.

PANIC IN PANAGIA

"I think he told us to go up this track and keep walking," Ron pointed as we crossed the river and turned inland from Galini's, "and we'll be in Panagia."

Panagia is one of the titles given to the Virgin Mary in Greek Orthodoxy; the deeply wooded area hiding against the hill which rises to Argalasti was so named in honor of her. Kalamos was well settled in Paleolithic times, but we will never know what it was called then and probably not even through the Neolithic, Bronze Age and Classical periods.

The vegetation became more dense as we walked along the narrow pathway and began to find ourselves in another world. Towering trees, planted who knows how long ago and by whom, provided a coolness in striking contrast to the still high September heat at the coast, only about a kilometer away. Plants I could not name brushed against our legs; we instinctively took care not to crush them. The spring flowers had long gone, their seeds waiting in the ground for their next turn while the winter flowers began to take the stage. The cyclamen that would put on a spectacular show once winter approached had begun almost timidly to bloom, tucked away amongst the roots of trees, as though checking that it was safe to come out. Birds and insects zipped and fluttered through the foliage to sip the water seeping here and there from the ground. Yet it seemed quiet. The strident screeching and squawking of the gulls at the shoreline was absent. No human voice intruded on the magic. A nymph or centaur might not have seemed out of place.

Long abandoned grape vines sashayed exuberantly with indigenous creepers and climbers, making it not only difficult to walk through in some parts, but enveloping forms so completely that one could only guess at what lay underneath. As we continued along the path, buildings of handcut stone became visible through the dense vegetation. Many of these were in complete ruin, some were still standing, but none were fully intact. Most no longer had doors. Their windows were small and few, gaping at our intrusion through empty frames. Surprisingly, the lintels in various windows and doors were mainly intact, perhaps because they were embedded in the stone structure and could not easily be removed and repurposed. Here and there roughly hewn beams of oak and chestnut jutted out at awkward angles from the walls, all that remained of missing roofs that had sheltered families. Several of these timbers were almost completely smothered by the vines that crisscrossed them, climbing to the light. Others lay fallen and rotting on the ground among the pieces of slate that had once kept out the rain. Elemental forces had wreaked havoc.

In contrast to the joyful atmosphere in Magda's little beachside home, open to the sea and bathed in light, Panagia had an air of melancholy about it, not helped by the tree canopy shutting out the sun. Oranges and lemons rotted in abundance around the wrecks of former homes where people had created their lives, and where surely laughter and song had played their parts in better days.

Vageli's recounting of Panagia's history had set the mood. He had told of the seaside inhabitants of Kalamos fleeing, panic-stricken, to her hidden shelter when pirates and marauders were spotted by the lookouts of old. He spoke of people continuously subjected to attack who had developed the refuge over hundreds of difficult years, taking valuable time away from the endless toil of daily life to do so. He spoke with warmth and enthusiasm, capturing our imaginations just as Homer did when he sang his verses in that time so very long gone by.

It was hard to reconcile the tranquility of the surroundings with the stress of the events experienced there through the ages. While I pondered the Panagia of former days, Ron was exploring the various ruins.

"Cathy, here. Look. It's an old olive pressing mill. Must go back a couple of hundred years or more. All done by man and beast … donkeys."

I moved with difficulty through the vegetation towards him, knitting in hand and entered the building. It was large, with a high vaulted roof. The construction was of rocks. Long wooden joists, placed at regular intervals between the layers of rocks, gave support as the walls were built up in height. Many of the beams were of great length, indicating how wooded the area must have been and how considerable a growing period the felled timber had enjoyed.

High up on the crudely whitewashed walls were a number of small apertures, window-like, with heavy iron bars across them, but with no glass. Perhaps they never did have glass and were intended only to let in light and air, or maybe any glass had been smashed by human hand or nature.

"This part was obviously the storage area. Look at these huge jars." There were several clay jars of the sort used in the past for olive oil, their graceful shape unchanged since archaic times. "So, after they'd pressed and collected the oil," Ron continued, "it would be put in these. Over there is the equipment they used to press out the oil."

We moved to another part of the building. The floor was thick with soil and some sort of material which looked like rotted vegetation.

"You can see how long this mill's been abandoned, Ron … so sad."

"Some of this is probably the pulp that's left after the oil has been squeezed out … skins and the crushed olive pits. It's used in various ways. I believe it can be dried for fuel, or for compost."

"Yes, but look at all this." Sundry items were strewn about. Old mattresses, ragged blankets, clothing, empty canned food tins, wine bottles, beer cans, the remains of fires. "People have been camping here in recent years. Living rough, Ron, whoever they were. Homeless. I wonder what the story is?"

Ron was still examining the machinery in the old mill. "There's practically a timeline here of how the oil's been extracted through the years. This system," he indicated two enormous stone wheels, "was worked by men or donkeys rotating these. A huge improvement on crushing the olives by hand. And this," he moved to a rusted contraption sitting atop a stone platform, "is a very early diesel-powered grinding machine."

I continued to knit, trying to appear interested, but my thoughts were carrying me back, far back in time as I imagined what daily life there must have been like. Not easy. No question of that, no matter whether the era was Neolithic, Bronze Age, Iron Age, modern age. All had their difficulties.

"I'm going to sit down there for a bit," I walked towards a fallen log. "I've got to sort out my knitting. You keep looking around, but be careful nothing falls on you."

He went off and I applied myself to a stitch that had been dropped several rows down. My mind began to wander. What little ancient history I knew rattled though my head as I tried to arrange the timelines involved in the life of the settlement. Those two enormous millstones tugged at my imagination. Their weight had to be considerable. How on earth were they made? When? Millstones have been used by various civilizations since at least the Neolithic Age. Could the millstones in Panagia be thousands of years old? "Ron! Ron! Where are you?"

"Over here. There's quite an orchard - must've been quite something at one time." Ron came into view through the undergrowth a little distance away from me.

"Ron, those millstones could be really ancient, couldn't they? Could they have been here for centuries?"

"No, I think these are fairly modern. Recently made. Probably within the last hundred years or so."

"But how can you know that?"

"Well, it looks like they were made to fit that metal bin thing they're in, so maybe they weren't just found lying about."

"But couldn't it be the other way round? That huge basin was made to fit the millstones?"

Ron smiled. "No, sorry Cathy, but I don't think we can deduce that. The building – that very high roof – was made to accommodate the system of pulleys in there. Those stones and that container were made to work together. That was a state-of-the-art olive mill in its time. Quite advanced technology actually."

"Was the coastline in the same position as now when Panagia was first peopled?" I asked.

"No, I reckon where we're now was much further inland in prehistory. The sea wasn't anywhere near as close. There'll have been a lot of erosion. Earthquake. Wave action. We can look up the history of Thessaly when we get the chance. I'm going to have another look at the equipment in that mill."

❖ ❖ ❖

I settled back down on my log and looked around. About thirty yards in front of me a large house was partially visible through a cluster of tall trees, with what seemed to be iron bars on the stone wall. I approached for a better look. The bars were set into the crumbling stones of the upper floor of the ruined dwelling, and were fixtures in a window. The window itself had lost any glass it once had. The roof had caved in, the debris piled up against the protective bars blocking any view into the space behind it. A shutter, one of a pair, hung at a crazed angle on the wall. There was no sign of the other which probably lay far down below, and completely engulfed by stone and vegetation. It was all so sad, so forlorn. Who had ensured that the home was well guarded against intruders, and when? The house was big. It had been added to over the years, as evidenced by single level structures attached on either side. These were built by other hands. Hands which had cut the rocks in a different manner. Hands which arranged the building stones forming the walls in a way that contrasted with those of the imposing building in the middle. Now the formerly secure home, safe and sturdy, had been breached by Nature herself, taking back her wood, her stone, her earth.

The settlement of Panagia had existed for aeons but today it lay abandoned, faintly breathing its ancient memories to those who could hear them. Suddenly aware of the heat, I made my way back through the plants and rubble to the familiar comfort of my knitting waiting on the log.

Shafts of light sliced through the trees as the sun moved higher into the sky. Oleanders, native to the Mediterranean region, had grown very tall in Panagia, their branches heavy with dark pink blooms which responded to the sun in dazzling brilliance. The birds seemed to become quieter, the insects more subdued as the effects of jet lag meshed with the rhythm of my knitting and my musings. Prehistory? What peoples were occupying this secluded spot then? Had they left any traces? And who came after them? Where did the Myceneans fit into the narrative? The land now called Panagia provided sanctuary for centuries from attacks by all manner of marauders, as it did to the terrified Greeks fleeing the more recent and brutal Nazi occupation during the Second World War.

A pair of bright blue butterflies twirled in front of me. Putting my knitting carefully down on the log I snapped a photo of them, but as I picked my work up again the yarn caught under a loose piece of bark, pulling it away from the log, to evict a large scorpion in the process. My shrieks shattered the stillness as I fled, the yarn trailing behind me. Ron hurtled through the vegetation.

"What is it? What's happened? Are you all right?"

"Get them off me! Get them off me!" I screeched, leaping from foot to foot, wildly brushing at my clothes.

"What? Where? I don't see anything?"

"Scorpions! Dozens of them! All over me!" I was teetering on the verge of hysteria.

"There! See! Look!" I hopped about, pointing at the ground in front of the log.

"Oh hell yes, I see," he replied, gazing at the mother scorpion frantically scuttling around in an attempt to retrieve her offspring. My dislodging the bark had exposed the sinister looking creature and the infants clinging to her back.

It took Ron quite a while to convince me that no repulsive critters had taken up residence on my person. Any unsuspecting soul wandering through Panagia would have been astounded at the sight of me stamping my feet and tearing my fingers through my hair as Ron methodically examined my clothes and the knitting. He was taken aback at my reaction, though he'd be the first to concede that close encounters of the scorpion kind aren't everyone's idea of fun.

"They eat them in Taiwan," he offered, unhelpfully.

"You may have, but just because you spent part of your weird childhood in Taiwan doesn't mean I have to like them. They're horrible! Ghastly!"

"Well no, I didn't eat any myself, but I saw others rather enjoying them … fried."

Taiwan's culinary tastes were of no interest to me. All I was concerned with was letting ma scorpion get on with her child rearing activities. As far away from me as possible.

Creepy crawly things don't usually bother me but scorpions I cannot stand. I cannot bear them. The little blighters seem so sneaky. So sinister. Those menacing pincers. The way they position that evil-looking tail and then hurl it so as to catch you unawares. Something about that really terrorizes me. They look armor-plated, like they're suited up for battle. I'd rather encounter a snake any day than a scorpion. And yet there the devoted mother was, giving her babies a piggyback until they were able to molt at least once and become independent of her.

Big Mama scorpion and her brood had destroyed my reverie though no harm was done, and Ron reported that she'd decamped with her babies to the shelter of a nearby rock. He picked up my knitting bag, shaking it out before putting my knitting inside it, while I jittered about.

"Why don't we go back? I think I've seen enough here for now."

Poor Ron didn't argue, instead feeding me chocolate to soothe my nerves as we left Panagia behind and headed to Magda's. But I'd lost my innocence, and still check for lurking scorpions under every rock and piece of wood, not to mention inside my shoes. I've yet to settle on a name for baby scorpions though. Scorplets? Scorplings? Whatever they may be called I hold no affection for them.

❖ ❖ ❖

We badly needed refreshment by the time we were walking past Bakaloni's on our way to Magda's so we paused to have a coffee. I'm not normally a coffee drinker, but tea at Bakaloni's was a most insipid herbal infusion which is widely drunk and called 'mountain tea'. Beloved by many, this tisane would undoubtedly have delighted Poirot but I do not do "floral notes." I'm a builder's tea kind of girl. Tea should revive one and not merely slake the thirst. In fact, now that I've got started on the subject I could climb on a soapbox about some tea an enthusiastic purveyor in the Adelaide Central Market persuaded us to buy at no inconsiderable cost.

"Buddha's tears," he called it. "The Queen drinks it."

Whether or not Her Majesty is partial to it, it certainly caused me tears and not merely because of the price, but rather because, once brewed, it resembled nothing more than a faintly green-tinged cup of hot water. How could Australian descendants of fellow Brits have sunk to such depths.

Anyway, I digress. Bakaloni wasted no time in pouring Ron an ouzo, something he always did when he saw us. I refrained from mentioning my encounter with that venomous predator and her progeny lest I should break out in an unseemly shaking and trembling. No need to be regarded as even more strange than already thought.

Having spent a polite interval with those good souls, we returned to Magda's to think about lunch. Mindful that we were to dine later at Galini's restaurant, we nibbled on bread and cheese followed by fresh fruit. I washed it down with tea - two Lipton's bags in a mug – and Ron, having already developed a taste for a Greek plonk that Bakaloni stocked, enjoyed a glass or two of the stuff. The European idea of a brief respite after lunch is most sensible, giving one the opportunity to contemplate one's role in the grand scheme of things, and a custom we took to most enthusiastically in the sleepy afternoon heat.

❖ ❖ ❖

The sun had begun its journey to light up the lives of others when we awoke. I'd fallen asleep in one of Magda's plastic reclining chairs, which I'd first carefully examined, and I did so again in case distant relatives of the scorplings had come to call. All clear. We freshened up, brewed more tea and prepared to take a slow walk across to the restaurant.

"Come on, Ron, what's taking you so long?"

"I need to find my flashlight," he responded, "or we'll be walking back in the dark."

Thinks of everything, Ron does, so once he was satisfied that he'd locked up, and I had my knitting bag in hand, we set off to retrace our steps of the morning.

We passed Bakaloni's where a couple of locals were enjoying a beer, and paused to exchange a few words, politely refusing Bakaloni's offer of a glass of ouzo.

Skirting the cars by Mrs-No-Parking's immaculately swept bit of the promenade, we proceeded towards the beach. Here the concrete ends abruptly, and a jump's required onto the rock-strewn sand in front of a disused olive mill. Walking towards us was a small man, sturdy of body, his face a deep mahogany from years of exposure to the sun and crinkled up by an enormous smile.

"*Kalispera*," he greeted us. "Good evening."

I could tell he was Albanian, one of the migrant workers who have contributed so much to Greece. He dug his hands into the pockets of his tattered trousers – his working clothes – and produced walnuts which he pressed upon us, beaming all the while and chattering away in his somewhat eccentric Greek. I am always in awe of adults who manage to learn a foreign language. What an accomplishment that is, and I have very little patience with any who would dare to mock their speech. And so we met Costa, an exceptional soul who has since become an important part of our lives.

DINNER FIT FOR THE GODS

Vageli and Eleftheria made us most welcome when we arrived. Vageli seated us at a table which he promptly covered with a paper tablecloth, adjusting it in place with plastic clips. There were a few other diners there who were obviously not Greeks. We heard English spoken as well as German, so we assumed that these were holiday makers like ourselves. Some of them were doing their best to speak in Greek to our hosts, and I was impressed by their attempts at the language which is by no means an easy one to pick up. Vageli was at pains to introduce us to English speakers, whom he obviously knew well. We soon learned that several of his patrons are regulars who have holiday homes in the area. They greeted us with good-natured remarks.

"Welcome to the best food in Pelion – no doubt about it!"

"Always absolutely delicious, no matter what you order."

"Nobody cooks like Eleftheria – not anybody."

"You'll love it here – they always make you feel like family."

The compliments flowed, and well deserved they were too.

Vageli placed a small basket containing bread and cutlery on our table, and handed us each a menu. With order book and pen in hand, he pointed out his recommendations from the fairly extensive list, and then described the specials of the day.

"Ah," said Ron, "I heard *calamari*. Right?"

Vageli nodded. "*Ne, ne,* yes." He explained that he had the typical *calamari* rings which we could have grilled or fried, but he also had stuffed *calamari.* "*Calamari gemisto.*"

"So Ron, you can have the *calamari* cut into the rings you're familiar with, or the body which is stuffed with whatever Eleftheria's recipe is and served like that. Vageli says we're lucky it's on the menu tonight."

"No contest, that's what I'm having, please tell him."

I did, and then chose the Greek meatballs for myself. "What about starters, Ron? The *meze*? They have a huge variety. We could skip the main dishes if you like and just get a selection of the *meze*."

Ron smiled at Vageli. "Why don't we just tell him to bring us a few different things to begin with, but I'm not giving up my *calamari*."

Vageli and I settled on white wine and he left to fetch it, returning a few minutes later with the jug of wine, a couple of glasses and a bowl of olives.

"I'll be back soon," and he went off to seat a group of people who had just arrived.

"They work hard, Ron, they really do. Eleftheria's on her own in the kitchen – no helper, cooking away in this heat. Only imagine what it must be like in the height of summer."

"So," Vageli returned to our table, "shall I bring you *horta*, *taramasalata* and *saganaki* to start?"

"Yes, please," I replied and turned to Ron. "You know what those are, right, you've had them before."

"Yes, *saganaki's* the fried cheese and *taramasalata's* that delicious dip. It's made with roe. But what's *horta*?"

"Greens. Chard. Dandelions and the like. Wild stuff. People gather it in the fields. Actually," I laughed, "some people call it weeds. But really it means leafy green vegetables. Boiled, and with olive oil and lemon dressing. Very healthy … very good for the kidneys, apparently."

Vageli arrived with the *meze* and two plates.

"Thanks, not yet," I told Ron as he prepared to give me a serving of *horta*, "I'll have the *horta* with my *keftedes*."

We took our time eating the *saganaki* and roe, enjoying the relaxed atmosphere in that most unassuming of tavernas. Diners finished their meals and left, or moved to chat with friends at other tables; Greek, English and German could be heard. Vageli bustled about all the while, arranging tables and chairs, clearing tables, taking orders, coming and going from the kitchen inside.

He brought my *keftedes*, accompanied by a large helping of crisply fried potato chips. "Yummy," I popped a second one in my mouth. "Have some Ron. Really tasty. They're handcut. You can tell they're not from a bag of frozen ones."

I helped myself to *horta*, and a few slices of tomato from the dish with the *keftedes*. "Right, that's me about to start eating. He'll bring yours soon."

In a small taverna like Vageli's it's not that easy to get everyone's meal cooked and on the table at the same time, but a few minutes later Vageli put a plate in front of Ron. The stuffed *calamari*, cut into thick slices and beautifully arranged on a bed of rice, surrounded by shredded carrot, cabbage, and lemon wedges arrived at our table. "Oh wow, Ron! I'm having some of that," and I immediately forked a piece over onto my plate. "Here, have a few meatballs."

The food was absolutely delicious. Isn't it amazing how the best food is often to be found in what might be called a hole-in-the wall? The rather nondescript surroundings of Galini's Taverna gave no indication of the culinary delights produced by Eleftheria. You had to be in the know.

❖ ❖ ❖

The pace began to slacken as people were served, and no others arrived in search of dinner. A few diners finished their meals and left, but several lingered over another beer, another bottle of wine. Cheerful conversations with Vageli and with each other flowed between the tables as news was exchanged and acquaintances renewed. A very pleasant atmosphere indeed.

"So tell me," Vageli set a plate with two chocolates and some peeled apple wedges on the table, "how was the food?"

"Superb!" I told him. "Excellent. And those meatballs ... what does Eleftheria put in them! Such flavor."

He pulled up a chair and sat down with us. "She's finishing in the kitchen and will come in a bit. You can ask her then."

We chatted a few minutes and then Eleftheria approached, wiping her hands on her ever-present apron.

"The meatballs, Eleftheria, were divine. Is the recipe a secret? What gives them that extra zest?"

"It's the meat. It's the mince. A mixture of pork and beef, that's essential. And then of course the *botana.*"

I nodded. "The herbs? I can taste parsley." I didn't push her further. Every Greek cook has her own favorite combination of herbs. Greece is a treasure house of herbs, a botanist's paradise, with literally hundreds of different varieties to be found in the fields and wild places. Some are native to certain islands only; many have become exceedingly rare. Generations upon generations of women have passed down their extensive knowledge of herbs to their families, both their culinary and their medicinal use.

"Did you go to Panagia?" Eleftheria asked. "I pick some of my herbs there. The people long ago had planted some very special ones. A few of them still grow in places. You have to know where to look though."

"Yes, we went. Thanks very much. We could never have found it on our own. It's very interesting. To think it goes back to ancient history." I didn't mention the eight-legged inhabitants with their pincers and their stingers, their many evil little eyes, and my terror of them.

"How long is it since the people left Panagia?" I asked them.

Eleftheria looked at Vageli. "After the war?"

"Yes, by the end of the Civil War they had gone." He was referring to the struggle between the Left and the Right that began during the Second World War, and which plunged the already devastated country into even greater post-war chaos and upheaval.

I explained very briefly to Ron, who said: "Ask them, please, who might have been living very rough there recently?"

"That was Albanians who came across the border into Greece after Communism collapsed in Albania. They had nothing there. They were here illegally. Without papers. They took any kind of work they could find. Panagia was a place to hide. The police wouldn't find them there."

The fall of Communism in the countries that had made up Yugoslavia, the wars and the suffering that ensued, were not subjects I wanted to get into right then. The ethnic cleansing and appalling human rights abuses of those conflicts were still occurring in parts at that precise period. I was very conscious of the ongoing horror; of the fact that I was safe and well fed, sitting in peaceful surroundings, listening to Greek music playing in the background. Distressing enough to discuss at any time, but not after the long day and the need to translate for Ron.

We chatted a little more but I wanted my bed, and was eager to get our body clocks fully adjusted to local time. It was already quite late, so we didn't linger too much longer. We paid up, said our goodbyes and promised to return soon to take coffee with them.

Walking back to the house by flashlight proved to be a slightly different proposition from the daylight stroll. Rocks had a tendency to retreat from view into the shadows, while pools of water lurked in the dark patches of sand. Crabs scuttled off to hide as we approached but they don't bother me, unlike scorpions. I lamented the fact that I knew so little about the habits of these prehistoric predators, and of course I couldn't have Googled them for more info. Just as well, for I now know that scorpions are mostly nocturnal – no wonder mother dear had been so irritated that her infants' naps had been disturbed – and they had first come to light about 430 million years ago.

HERMES AND EMAIL

Apollo had long since pulled his sun chariot across the sky when we awoke. The previous day had been packed with incident and our bodies were reminding us of that.

"I'll put the kettle on, Cathy, and get some tea into you."

"Thanks, but it's going to take a lot of caffeine if I'm to function at all this morning."

We sat sipping our tea and coffee in the courtyard while the gulls swooped back and forth, their strident cries so at odds with the twittering of the flycatchers as they darted through the olives and the oleanders. The sea lapped at our feet, as though gently to remind us of her presence.

The Greek gods had Hermes to act as their messenger, and mighty busy he was, but we had no Internet and no data networks in Kalamos in those days. The cost of making calls to Texas on a cell phone was crippling, so we needed to establish some form of rudimentary communications.

Ron's behavior had become increasingly odd. Well, more than usual for he'd leave the table and wander about, holding the cell phone up in the air and muttering to himself. At times he would stand still, examining the screen intently, taking steps to the left, then swinging to the right.

"You choreographing a ballet?" I grinned. "Are you trying to touch base with Hermes? He has those wings on his sandals and a cute little tunic. Will you be wearing a tutu?"

"Very funny. I'm looking for a signal. Surely you want to get your emails?"

He had a point.

"I'm going up the hill - it's blocking any signal I might be able to get. There'll be better reception if I go higher."

I followed him, knitting in hand, along the rock-strewn, ankle-turning trail to the top of the hill where the view across the Gulf to Volos and the mountain is open and unimpeded by any structure. Ron was weaving between the olive trees that line the cliff edge, holding the Nokia phone aloft.

"Right, I'm getting a reasonable signal from the tower in Volos. Stay here. I'll run down to the house and fetch the laptop. Won't be long."

He returned a few minutes later with the laptop, his notebook and a pen. The seagulls, those most quarrelsome of creatures, were having a slanging match overhead while Ron crouched at the base of a large olive tree.

"Can you hold this steady, please?" He positioned the laptop carefully among the intertwined olive roots, then stood up pointing the Nokia towards Volos.

I clutched the laptop, nervous of the curious gulls diving in for a closer look. I kept thinking of Hitchcock. His birds didn't have a clue how to do menacing, and could have used some lessons from these guys.

Ron took the computer and connected it to a cable he had in his pocket. The other end was plugged into the phone, which he wedged between two branches of the tree. A few minutes later he grinned. "Got the emails! Let's go to the house and read them."

I was amazed, but then I always am if it's anything to do with computers. As far as I'm concerned pushing a button and having something work is nothing short of a miracle. I made tea while Ron typed away on the laptop at the courtyard table.

"Here, come and read your mail. You can write whatever you want, and then I'll go back up and send them."

"But how are you doing it? I don't understand."

"I arranged for a special AT and T number when we left Austin – that gives me dial up access to the internet through Thessaloniki. I can't do it from here – the house is down in this hollow. I can't get a signal. That's why I have to go up the hill where I have line of sight to Volos."

Hermes may well have been swift, moving from the world of the Olympian gods to that of the mortals with ease, but Ron had made it possible for us to communicate between our remote little corner of Kalamos and the great big world beyond. At least twice a day we walked up to the venerable old olive tree and there, high above the Pagasitic Gulf, Mt. Pelion observed us in silence as we sent and received messages that seemed to be carried only by the wind. Marconi would have been impressed.

"I'm going to send these emails. You don't need to come unless you want to."

"I'll come with you," I packed my knitting into its bag, "but I'm going to stay for a bit. It's so lovely up there."

"OK, but I'll come back here. I've got some technical papers to read." Ron put a bottle of water in my bag. "Here, you'll need this. It's getting hot."

We set off. We were probably rather an odd sight, but who was likely to see us, and who was even likely to care?

"The emails have been sent. Are you sure you'll be alright?" Ron put the phone back into his pocket and prepared to return to the house.

"Go, go, I'm perfectly fine." Settling back against a large olive tree where I'd stationed myself, I waved him off.

❖ ❖ ❖

From my vantage point the Pagasitic spread itself out like an infinite sheet of hand-dyed blue silk. Variations in tone shimmered from its depths. Indigo and turquoise, shot with purple. Not a wave on the sea. Not a cloud in the sky. The mainland directly across from me in the west was an undulating series of mountains and hills against the horizon, gleaming a dark green in the sunlight. To my left small islands which I could not name, about which I had as yet no knowledge, appeared to float upon the water.

To my right stood the mountain, Pelion, known since antiquity, the densely wooded home of centaurs, and summer playground of the Olympian gods. Below it lies Volos. From the ancient city of Iolkos, part of which modern Volos now occupies, Jason and his men set sail on their ship, the Argo, to secure the Golden Fleece. And from here Thessalian warriors set sail to support Agamemnon in his attack on Troy, taking with them superior horses from the plains of Thessaly.

The Greek myths, the dramatic stories of heroes, Aesop's wise fables - these were my bedtime stories, told in modern Greek. My Mother sometimes recited Homer's thrilling tales to me in ancient Greek, the gentle sound soothing me to sleep, not that I understood it. Perhaps she too found it comforting. I never thought to ask her why she was so well-versed in these epic poems. Were they learned by rote as part of her schooling? Or did she so love the words, the rhythm, the cadence that she'd committed large sections of Homer to memory? I will never know.

A red-painted *caïque* came into view around the headland, the distinctive sound of its diesel engine competing with the frenzied calls of the ever present gulls hoping for scraps of fish. A man on deck was paying out the nets while another was just visible at the wheel inside a little cabin. The sight and the noise are familiar ones, for Greeks have built these wooden fishing boats by hand since antiquity. They are part of Greek culture. They can be found depicted on ancient pottery, on friezes, in mosaic floors. These classic vessels carried people and their animals, their goods and chattels, and still do, particularly in the islands where they are often the only means of connection between them. The design of the *caïque* has changed very little through the millennia, except for the mast and sails which have been replaced by the inboard diesel engine. The lives of their owners aren't likely to be easy ones though. A wooden boat needs constant maintenance. Any time spent on repairs means income lost. It must always have been so.

The men on the *caïque* waved back to me. I wished them well, hoping the catch would be a good one, though of course I made no attempt to shout my greetings to them. The rumbling and the clacking of their engine, not to mention the racket from the gulls, made it impossible to be heard. The *caïque* and its crew moved across the Gulf. I watched them, knitting all the while, as they and their ever-present winged followers disappeared further around the coast.

It was beginning to get quite hot. The sun was high in the sky, from which I deduced it was about noon, but I hadn't clue as to the actual hour for I'd no idea what Daylight Savings in Greece was doing with God's good time.

Just as I began to think of returning to Magda's cool courtyard, Ron appeared at the top of the hill. "I'm coming to get you. I've put together something that can pass for lunch. Up you get."

He pulled me to my feet and we walked together along the pebbly footpath to the house.

The meal Ron had prepared more than passed for lunch. Having finished mine, I got up to take the plates through to the kitchen. "How are we doing for supplies?" I asked on my return.

"We are very low, actually. We didn't get much the other night."

We hadn't really shopped for food. The earthquake had distressed us greatly, and we hadn't lingered in Argalasti.

"Unless we go out today, Cathy, we have no yoghurt for breakfast tomorrow. We need milk. And bread … we always need bread." He grinned at me. "The gulls get more bread than I do."

"When will we go? Everything will be closed now … will open again around 5 p.m."

"The closing's a good idea, though. Think about it, Cathy. They start early … rest in the heat of the day … open up when it's beginning to cool down."

"So what are you suggesting? We go buy something to cook for tonight?"

"We can. Do you want to eat somewhere in Argalasti? There's tavernas there."

"Ron, let's just play it by ear then. Depends on what we find. We can always go back to Vageli's. Who really wants to cook now?"

HUNTING FOR FOOD

A lazy afternoon passed very pleasantly. I sorted out the various knitting projects, putting each into a bag with the appropriate yarn and needles; that way I could easily choose which to work on in the car, and while exploring. Serious knitters will identify with this system. You need something simple to work on when you can't devote your undivided attention to the project. More intricate patterns, and especially if there's a lot of colorwork requiring many different yarns, are usually best done when interruptions are few. And nothing's more disconcerting when you're away from your collection of knitting tools than to discover you've reached a point where a different needle's required, and you haven't got it with you. I can, so to speak, become quite unraveled.

"We can go up anytime you're ready," Ron said as he brought me a mug of tea. "No rush. Places will be opening about now."

"Look, the sea's sort of coming to life." Little waves had begun rippling the water which had been serene all day. "Do you think the weather's changing?"

Ron studied the sky. "No clouds I can see. A slight breeze is all. Probably something to do with the temperature dropping as the sun goes down."

We took our time over the tea, then tidied up a little and headed for the car. She of the "You can't park here" mantra had actually nodded at us the previous day, but we hadn't pushed our luck, and kept the Elantra away from her fiefdom.

The road to Argalasti was an unpaved dirt track. It was also something of an obstacle course, for the potholes which riddled it laid many a trap for the unwary. Driving on it was often further enlivened by encounters with sheep, shepherds and dogs. These were far less difficult to handle than the cascades of goats which would engulf the car in a maelstrom of multi-colored coats, their horns tossing about in clouds of dust as they climbed and clambered over each other to reach into trees and vegetation, their piercing eyes quite unnerving. Sheep behave in a different manner, thronging together in a tight mass while you edge along past them.

We reached Argalasti without incident and parked in front of the church at the main crossroads. An old fellow was sitting on the low wall near the bus stop, a box of tomatoes for sale alongside him. "Ron, look. Let's buy from him. They're so red and knobbly. Not shop perfect. Means he grew them, don't you think? Hopefully no poisons."

We selected some. Ron counted out the drachma in bills and coins. No Euros yet at that time. The amounts seemed staggering. Paying for a few tomatoes in hundreds if not thousands of drachma seemed unreal to me. The tomato-man wrapped them up individually in old newspaper and then put them in a well-used paper bag. He went to a lot of trouble for a very small amount of money; I was quite touched. Ron put them in the car and then we walked across to the tiny supermarket.

"Shall go to the bakery first, Ron? We could get some nice bread and then maybe cold meat and cheese from the supermarket. Sandwiches tonight?"

"No, I'd rather have a proper meal. Get what you want and we'll look for a taverna where we can eat."

I chose a multi-grain loaf and was thrilled to find it still warm, and a plain white loaf for the gulls.

"Those gulls will sure miss you when we're gone."

"Maybe, but not as much as I'll miss this *baklava*."

The lady who served us smiled as she handed me the beautifully wrapped box, tied with ribbon.

The supermarket wasn't very big, but it had a reasonable selection of tinned and packaged food items, a comprehensive dairy section, a small but perfectly adequate variety of cold meats, plenty of cleaning materials and sanitary products, various pet foods, together with several of the small odds and ends a household might require. Argalasti had two pharmacies, two butchers, a hardware business, a liquor store, and sundry greengrocers who operated out of roadside stalls.

"We're well supplied, at least for the time being," I placed our various purchases in the car. "Is there still something special we can get?"

"You know what I would like?" replied Ron as we walked up from the church towards the square. "I'd really love some beef, or maybe lamb, but that someone else has cooked. I smell meat grilling somewhere. Let's look around a bit."

We crossed the square. People were sitting in the open at an assortment of tables, enjoying a drink or meal being brought to them from whichever eatery it had been ordered at. Children were running about in the age-old way that kids do all over the world. It was a bit breezy but nothing bad enough to drive you indoors.

"Over there." Ron pointed to a neatly lettered sign indicating that the establishment within, by name of "Artemis", specialized in grilled meats. "Let's give it a try? Do you mind?"

Why would I? The owner approached us immediately as we entered, greeting us in English and making us feel very welcome. We were seated at a well-placed table in a quiet corner, handed menus and asked what we'd like to drink. We agreed on a white wine, one of the local varieties, which was very soon brought to the table, together with a plate of olives. Visible from inside was a glassed-in area, rather like a smokehouse, where the meats were prepared. It was well-appointed with a rotisserie and other equipment, and led directly into the kitchen. A very good arrangement indeed.

"What should we have? There's lamb and pork, sausage and *souvlakia*, but the emphasis is on meat and salads. Not so much on prepared dishes."

"Nice," I replied, studying the vegetables listed. "I'm having potato salad, and a *horiatiki*, of course. Meat dish? I don't know. Lamb cutlets look good."

"Horiatiki, definitely. Nothing like it. Can you ask them to give us extra *feta*, please? I think I'll ask for a mixed grill platter. It's written here in English on the menu."

The young waiter came over and I discussed our choices with him. "No problem," he assured me and went off to the kitchen. He returned almost immediately with a plate of *feta* slices which he put down in front of Ron. "Please tell him that he won't go short of *feta* in his salad, but he can always ask for more."

We sat chatting over our wine.

"Ron, do you think it's called Artemis because she was the goddess of hunting? You know, with meat being their specialty?"

"Well, she was the goddess of many other things too, but yes, probably because of the meat. Unless it's maybe his wife's name or something."

Inside the smokehouse the owner was tending to the grilling. Our waiter went in and collected a large metal dish filled with meat which he took back into the kitchen, and soon he emerged with a tray which he placed on an empty table next to ours.

"That really looks good," Ron said, as the young man put the bread basket and cutlery in the middle of our table, and our plates in front of us.

And it certainly was. The mixed grill platter was huge – I needn't have ordered any other meat for myself – and was filled with lamb cutlets, pork chops, pancetta and three kinds of sausage. Together with the very large Greek salad, the potato salad and all the extra *feta*, we dined very handsomely. And as if we hadn't done well enough, a dish of the tiniest, most delicious chocolates, filled with ice-cream, arrived at our table, together with the bill. Ron added a generous tip and we rose to leave.

Our smiling host came over to thank us and escort us out, and was very surprised to be addressed in Greek. He immediately asked me what part of Greece I was from. Not Greek-born, I had to tell him, but born in Scotland to a Greek mother and a Scot. He was anxious to talk further but the place was beginning to fill up and he was far too busy. We said our goodbyes and left, with him urging us to come back soon to grace his taverna.

As we walked across the *plateia,* the central square of Argalasti, I spotted racks of magazines and newspapers outside of a little shop. "Hang on, Ron, I'm going to look at these."

There were several Greek newspapers, some German ones which were a few days out of date, and a two-week-old copy of The Times. What interested me though was the selection of guidebooks, maps, postcards and the like, with most of those available in Greek, English and German editions.

"These will be very useful," I said as we paid up and headed back to the car. "We'll get a good idea of what to go see." I opened the car door. "Oh gosh, do you think the milk and yoghurt will be OK? It's still quite warm out here."

"I thought of that. That's why I covered the bag with my jacket. As long as we put it straight into the fridge at Magda's it'll be fine."

BOREAS IS VERY ANNOYED

It was very dark once we'd left Argalasti and were driving down to Kalamos. Speckled here and there on the hills were the dim lights of a few houses, and the light from a couple of streetlamps along the road. The gloom didn't bother us at all. The night sky was clear of any cloud, and so illuminated by the moon and the stars in their trillions that white caps could be seen on the darkly purple sea.

"Do you see that, Ron? There are quite big waves on the water. The wind must be getting stronger."

"Well, it's certainly picking up speed, but I'm not going to look just yet. I'm not used to this road."

By the time we reached the sharp right turn onto the beachfront of Kalamos the waves could clearly be seen, racing in great swells down the coast. I opened the window to the sound and smell of the sea. Deep troughs frilled with white foam surged by, their rhythmic movement making me think of those hairstyles, the Marcel wave, worn by the glamorous film stars of cinema's early days.

"Well, it's coming out of the north. I've no idea what it means for the weather. No sign of any storm though. Let's get back to the house."

"Did we leave anything outside, Ron?"

"No, I don't think so, and anyway Magda's place seems to be quite protected."

To some extent yes, her house was well sheltered by the headland against which it was built, and the flow of the water usually swept past the tiny beach and not directly onto it. It was not possible to ignore the wind though. We struggled as we walked head on into it from the car, carrying our groceries along the sand and stones until we turned into the courtyard. The olive trees were bowed down to the ground, scattering their unripened fruit in all directions. The bougainvillea and oleander scratched and clawed against the roof tiles, which I was convinced were going to be hurled to the ground by the gale. "Quickly Ron, get the door open please!" I shouted through the wind as the shutters banged back and forth.

While I washed the milk and yoghurt containers in the stone sink, Ron managed to secure the shutters by means of the little latches screwed into them, but they weren't a tight enough fit; the shutters squeaked and scraped all through the night. The wind didn't let up for a second and neither did I, spending a pretty much sleepless night thinking of what might be occasioned by the relentless blustering. I was convinced we'd lose electricity – we didn't. Of course, the roof was never going to stay in place – it remained perfectly intact. I just knew that a great ancient olive tree would fall on the house – none did. I do a pretty good line in worrying.

By daybreak Boreas, Greek god in charge of the North Winds, was in no mood to be placated. Known for his bad temper, he did nothing to control his winds and instead kept up a steady gale right through that day and into the night.

We made tea and drank it in the cozy kitchen. Ron went outside to inspect for any damage, but aside from the battered bougainvilleas he found none. "I'm going up to the email tree," he said when he came back in. "I hope I can get the mail, but I want you to stay here. The wind's likely to be worse up there in the open."

I was in no mood to argue. "I'll get breakfast started, but please be careful." By the time I'd arranged bowls of yoghurt and cereal, and cut up a bit of fruit Ron was back.

"It's really rough up there. It's a straight line wind and there's nothing much to stop it. You'd not have coped, Cathy, it would've blown you right over. It was hard enough for me to stand. Anyway, don't ask me how but I managed to get the email."

We stayed in the kitchen after breakfast, doing email and reading. I tried to catch up on my knitting notes. Magda's had no sitting room inside and there was absolutely no need for one. Who would sit indoors when the courtyard was so comfortable, so pleasant with the sea and the birds to soothe anyone's soul? A quick glance through the door showed no change. No small boat dared to be on the water. The gulls were fewer in number, though some skittered over the waves in search of fish. I wondered where the rest were and determined to see if I could find any nests when we could walk along the cliffs and dunes again.

By late morning I was beginning to get bored cooped up indoors. "Tell you what, why don't we waddle across to Vageli's and find out what's going on?"

"It's a bit far in this wind, Cathy, it won't be a nice walk. Let's go see what's happening at Bakaloni's. We can buy you some chocolate."

The wisdom of Ron's words soon became apparent. The few hundred yards between Bakaloni and Magda had us doing a Lawrence of Arabia across the sand, and we were glad to get inside out of the stinging wind.

"Po! Po!" *Kyria* Katina exclaimed as we sort of blew in. "Are you alright? Is anything wrong? Do you need the telephone?"

Bakaloni, a man of few words, was already pouring Ron an ouzo. I took out my knitting, requested a coffee and soon we were chatting away.

"What is this wind? Does it happen often?"

"This is the Meltemi," they told me. "The Meltemi. It comes from Turkey."

Frankly I'd have preferred for it to stay there

"At certain times of the year it's quite common, yes. It's a dry wind. It usually doesn't bring rain, but it's very bad for the boats," continued Bakaloni.

"And in the winter it's horribly cold," added *kyria* Katina, with a little shiver, "and it can blow non-stop for days."

I explained to Ron.

"Like the Mistral then. Cathy, please ask them if they think it will last long. They might have an idea of the weather patterns."

The Bakaloni's debated for a little while, expressing the opinion that it would probably not last beyond the next day.

"*Avrio*," they said, "tomorrow it will be gone. By afternoon it will have left."

We drank more coffee, Ron was persuaded to have another ouzo, we bought chocolate, and took our leave.

"Avrio can't come soon enough," I grumbled as we bowed our heads into the wind. "Bring on tomorrow."

HEADING SOUTH

By the next morning the wind had indeed begun to subside, and the sea, though still a little choppy, was much calmer.

I'd spent the previous afternoon taking a good look through the guidebooks. "There's a huge amount to see, Ron. I don't really know where we should start." We were lingering over breakfast in the courtyard, the Meltemi trying to make up its mind whether to go or hang about. It seemed to have run out of energy, having only enough strength to puff a little.

"Let me look," Ron took the map of Pelion from me. It was my kind of map, not overly complicated, a map for the tourist. Places of interest were marked, the villages named and their attractions listed, ancient sites, churches and monasteries, beaches. Comprehensive, clear and colorful.

"Here we are. See? Kalamos. And up here is Argalasti. So Panagia is about here. This, where we are now, is the first little headland – where we get the email. Up here. You can see how protected Magda's house is. Then this second headland," he pointed to the map, "is the one we look across at from the email tree. Where we have that wonderful open view of Volos and the mountain."

"And there's a lovely little bay between these headlands. I've seen a *caïque* fishing in there while you're doing the email. We should maybe walk over there soon."

"Right, but I'm thinking we should explore a bit in the south today, Cathy. We drive up to Argalasti, turn right and then go down the road to wherever we feel like."

"Good plan. You'll drive, right? I didn't get an International License."

"There was really no need to. Anyway, you can knit and keep an eye on the map and stuff. Navigate. Let's clear up here and we can leave when you're ready."

The Meltemi had caused some damage. Aside from the litter that had been blown all over the place, we noticed quite a few broken branches, mainly olives, as we drove up towards Argalasti.

"Oh Ron, that's too bad," I said as we dodged a large branch lying forlorn amidst the leaf debris, "I hate that some farmer's lost good olives there."

We reached the main road, turned right, and a magnificent view of the Gulf appeared in front of us as we drove downhill. Down towards the tip of the Peninsula. Although the wind had subsided, the sea was still rather agitated. The Meltemi had unsettled it, had greatly disturbed its tranquility of the last few days. The only good thing it seemed to have done was blast the dry summer dust out, giving us a perfectly clear view across the Pagasitic to the mountainous mainland in the west.

"Mt. Parnassus is over there, Cathy. Delphi and the oracle. I'm really keen to see it. We'll take a day or two soon and go there."

Every shade of blue shimmered in the finely pleated water. It was like looking at the palette of an artist seeking the perfect tint for his canvas. Picasso and his Blue Period came to mind, and he did indeed love the sea, the Mediterranean, which had influenced his work.

There wasn't much traffic on the road, perhaps because of the time of day, but also because the holiday season was essentially over. We passed a small truck towing a trailer in which a very irritated goat was tethered to the side railing. There were crash barriers at places on the seaward side of the road, with crash being the operative word given the state of some of them. If one was inclined towards forensic analysis, much could be revealed by skid marks, the destruction to the barrier and the paint colors smashed into it, and the mess of broken glass and debris left by a damaged vehicle.

❖ ❖ ❖

At one point in the road we encountered an older woman seated sidesaddle on a donkey. Not, mind you, on the well-worn, narrow footpath alongside, but firmly in the road. Originally an ancient walking trail, the road had only very recently been tarred and extended, and would have been a well-used *kalderimi* in the good lady's childhood.

Ron immediately slowed to a crawl. "I'm going to creep past her, Cathy. I don't know what might come tearing along, and I don't want to spook the donkey."

The donkey didn't turn a hair. Neither did its rider, who sat atop the beast with all the aplomb of a ruler surveying her lands. As we drove behind her, I took as much note as I could of her clothing and paraphernalia, and used my camera to get a few shots. I didn't feel comfortable doing that – she might well not have liked it – but she couldn't see me and we could hardly stop to ask her permission.

"I've never seen a saddle like that, Ron. Have you?"

"Can't say as I have, but I'm not going to take a close look now."

The lady of the donkey wore her hair in two very long gray braids which reached to below her waist. A black scarf was wrapped around her head. Although autumn was approaching the weather was still very warm, but the Meltemi of the previous two days had afforded some relief from the heat. Perhaps she felt the cooler air more than we did, for she was wearing a baggy hand-knitted cardigan of rather indeterminate color and age. Her tiny feet, neatly crossed against the side of the donkey, poked out from under her long skirts. Thick black socks crumpled over her tattered shoes, tied with string for laces.

Ron inched past her. I waved. She smiled, inclining her head in acknowledgment.

"That really was something to see, Ron. I wonder how old she is? I'd love to talk to her. Imagine what she could tell us."

We continued downhill, the sea always in view. The road began to level out and carried us across a bridge spanning a little river, where a signboard welcomed us to Horto. To the left of the bridge the river was very thickly lined with tall reeds and other plants. To the right the river, running on down to the shore, and clear of any vegetation, widened, kept in check by concrete embankments. Small boats and *caïques* fastened to rings in the canal walls, bobbed up and down as though eager to head out to sea, their bright paintwork creating a kaleidoscope in the sunlit water. Together with the brilliant colors of oleander and bougainvillea, roses and lush greenery blazing all around in the tidy gardens of white-painted houses, the effect was striking. Here and there placards and notices indicated various accommodations available for rent, though many of the buildings appeared to be fully closed.

❖ ❖ ❖

The road continued downhill, leveling out as we reached Milina. Unlike Horto which had seemed quietly laid-back on that initial impression, Milina was bustling. The road runs along between the waterfront and the numerous buildings on the opposite side. Location is the reason why Milina attracts more attention. It's right on the beaten track. It's cheerful. There are restaurants, coffee shops, snack bars, ice cream stalls, vending machines. There are greengrocers, their fruit and veg selections enticingly laid out. There are shops and kiosks selling caftans and sarongs, sunhats and sandals, beach towels, beach toys, maps, guide books, newspapers, postcards and magazines. Even then, on our first look at Milina, with the holiday season coming to an end the waterfront had a most inviting air. It's obvious why it's such a popular resort. There's no denying that the commerce is more or less typical of any tourist destination, but in spite of the vacationers it retains an old world air with its beautiful church, the handsome older buildings and their wrought iron balconies. The Greek spirit of *filoxenia* – love of the stranger – is a deep-rooted part of the Greek culture. The concept of respect for strangers, of hospitality, goes back to the most ancient of times. The Greek myths tell of Zeus, that complex king of the Olympian gods, and his role as protector of guests and strangers.

"Should I park? You want a quick coffee?"

"No thanks, Ron, then I'd need to make a pit stop somewhere. This map doesn't show much in the way of more villages along the coast. Perhaps on our way back?"

We drove slowly on. The road began to empty as we moved away from the main center of activity. Buildings thinned out. Expanses of vacant land alongside the water provided parking space for the fishermen we saw dotted about, intent on their rods and nets, hoping for a decent catch. Some of these anglers were well set up under umbrellas or trees, seated on camping stools with cooler boxes at their side, presumably to receive the fruits, or should that be the fish, of their labors. At least some of those cooler boxes, I suspected, had a beer or two in them.

We noticed various boats secured to buoys along the coast. There were also a few pulled up on land, most of them turned upside down. Some seemed to have been abandoned, for their condition was poor and they were not seaworthy. Weeds had grown up around them. Wind-blown garbage was deposited against them. They could probably tell interesting tales.

Further along we came to a boatyard on the left, opposite a small harbor with many vessels at their moorings. The boatyard looked busy, with boats being repaired and painted. There's apparently nothing quite like a boat to demand constant attention - and I vaguely remembered the expression "messing about in boats", which of course bugged me until I could look it up much later. It comes from *The Wind in the Willows*, and has established itself firmly in the language since the book was first published in 1908. Strangely enough, I still have my battered copy of this children's classic but without my dictionary of quotations, I would never have remembered it.

❖ ❖ ❖

The further south we drove, the more uninhabited the area became. The sprinkling of buildings we saw near the road were either closed up securely for the winter, or completely abandoned, long unused.

"Ha, that's funny. There, that little sign, Ron. See? It's pointing the way to Kottes. That means chickens. Does it mean there're chickens there? Like for sale? Or is it a place?"

"Funny name for a place, isn't it? Wonder why?"

I never did find out how it got its name, but Kottes is indeed a place. A tiny, tiny, utterly gorgeous place, right on the sea. It has a couple of fish tavernas, and a few places to rent where you can while your summer vacation away in the most serene of surroundings. In winter though it's practically deserted. Almost everything's closed up and only fishing *caïques* come to call.

The landscape opened up as we carried on driving. Great tracts of rock-strewn terrain plunged down to the sea, the sky soaring into infinity above the expanse of water. For an instant my eye perceived the ground as moving, but the heaving mass was goats, dozens of them with their shaggy coats of black, gray, brown, white, milling about the exhausted earth in a frenzied horned and hairy scramble for the meager vegetation.

"That seems to be some kind of farm down there," I pointed to a ramshackle collection of buildings sprawled against a little rise. Not a soul was visible though there must have been people tending to the flocks grazing in the vicinity. "The view across the water, Ron, just look at it!"

"Let me stop. We can take some photographs." He parked the Elantra on the side of the road and we got out. "We need to stretch our legs anyway."

At first glance the structures appeared haphazard but a closer inspection revealed a degree of order in the construction.

"Those fenced parts there are pens. And those are milking sheds. Can you see the containers for the milk? And over there," Ron swept his arm across, "is where they store the hay and whatever other feed they use. They must have to supplement the grazing … there's no winter rains yet."

"It seems quite an operation then."

"Oh yes, there's a lot of milk being produced here. It may look a bit messy because of all the corrugated iron and the stone walls, but they've made use of whatever was available – those wood pallets are doing a good job in the gates and fences. Why waste them?"

We were told later that feta cheese is manufactured in small quantity by the farmers there, and excellent cheese it is too, with those in the know making the trip down to buy it. The goats are well tended, each having the ear tags that denote they comply with government regulations, and each one wears a bell around its neck.

The land and hills were brown, the ground baked and cracked, dry and dusty for summer was almost over though you'd never think so for the heat. "It's the equinox in a few days, right

Ron? So autumn's about to arrive. Then the rains come. I bet it gets really miserable down here in winter."

We got back in the car and moved off.

"It's like another world. Barren." Ron was referring to the dark cliffs that began to tower above us to the east, blocking much of the sunlight. The rocks, almost as old as time itself, rise jagged and threatening, piles of boulders and broken trees attesting to landslides. Deep ravines dense with vegetation scar its surface. I shivered. A moonscape, Ron calls it. The road twists along the cutting, and below it the rock falls away in strange, dark gray sheets to tattered coves where wind and wave toss the world's garbage out of the sea. Tenacious olive trees cling to crevices. Goats scrabbled about in their self-assured way, their piercing eyes alarming any onlooker who might find his vehicle surrounded by throngs of them choking the road, not to mention how startling it is to see a goat perched high in a tree.

Then suddenly the road curves to leave the crags behind, and bursts out above a vastness of sky and water that might leave you lost for words. Every shade of blue you can name surrounds you in fair weather; every shade of gray when the sky is sulking.

I don't think I've ever seen a goat without its bell, and you'll hear the jingle and the jangle as a herd appears with the accompanying sheepdogs. The turbulent flood of animals is accompanied across the lands by the herders, some on foot, some on horseback mounted sideways on a handmade wooden packsaddle. The herders will often have a cell phone in the hand that's not holding reins, or wielding a crook. The modern is literally hand in hand with the ancient.

◆ ◆ ◆

We continued to Agia Kyriaki, the southernmost of the coastal villages, where we spent time wandering through its port. Here fishing boats and other craft assemble to be repaired and made seaworthy again by craftsmen who continue the venerable traditions of their forefathers. The village boasts some of the best fish tavernas on the entire Peninsula, and although it's quite a long way from Volos it's packed with families at weekends and feast days during the warmer months.

From here the fishermen can easily exit the Gulf and ply through the channel to the open seas. Fresh seafood is always on the menu, and yet some visitors will ignore the variety on offer in favor of the ever-available *souvlaki*, or a pork chop. We sat at a table, literally inches from the water, under a huge canvas awning to wait for our food, and watched a fisherman mend his nets. So weather beaten was he that I couldn't hazard a guess as to his age. I struck up a conversation with him while Ron made short work of his *calamari* dish, and learned that his ancestors for as far back as he knew had lived and fished there. "Where else would I live?" was his simple comment.

There's something about Agia Kyriaki that infuses one with such a sense of relaxation that time seems suspended. And no, it's not in any way due to a glass or two of the local vino, for mindful that he has to drive Ron will not drink with the meal. We lunched like kings, and then made our leisurely way back to Kalamos to take up our positions at Magda's table with a chilled jug of wine to keep us company.

"Well, we didn't stop at Milina, so we'll drive back down soon and maybe have lunch on the promenade."

"Sounds a plan, but let's make it a dinner rather, Ron. It says here in the guidebook that Milina has wonderful sunsets."

"Nothing wrong with the sunset right here."

Indeed there wasn't. The sun, across the water from us, had begun sliding further and further toward the horizon, putting on a magnificent display of gold and crimson that streaked the sea and skies as the twilight made its appearance. The night sky gradually welcomed its stars which glittered with a startling intensity. An owl hooted nearby. Dogs barked in the distance. Ron looked up from his maps of Greece and refilled my glass.

"Isn't tomorrow when Magda's supposed to come?"

"What do you mean?"

"Well, didn't what's-his-name say when they were fixing the toilet, that she'd be here tomorrow to clean the house and change the linens?"

"Ah, yes, right … it is tomorrow that she's coming. Gosh Ron, the days are flying past. We'd better make sure we wake up early so we're ready."

"Do we have to stay while she's here, do you think?"

"I don't see why, but it might be interesting to talk to her. We'd better get sorted out here and get to bed then," I said, gathering up my knitting to follow Ron inside. We closed the door on the sea and a perfect day.

MEETING MAGDA

Shortly after sunrise my knitting and I were to be found at the courtyard table while Ron attended to the intricacies of making tea and coffee on the gas plate in the little kitchen. These tabletop appliances come in various configurations and are quite popular whether the home has electricity or not, though I must admit cooking with gas makes me nervous. Magda's had two burners – a large one for cooking and a tiny one for making coffee, Greek style, in the classic *briki*. This is a small pot with a long handle in which the coffee, water and sugar are boiled together; spices, notably cardamon may be added. The process requires bringing the coffee mixture to a rapid boil, removing it from the flame and bringing it back to the boil. This will be done a number of times according to the taste of the drinker, and requires some dexterity to avoid a messy spill.

Greeks can get quite passionate when discussing where this method of coffee brewing originated. I once made the mistake of referring to it as "*Turkiko*" coffee – Turkish coffee - and was very quickly corrected.

"We, we the Greeks, taught the Turks how to make coffee," sniffed an elderly gentleman whose long departed parents were certainly born when the Turks were still present in Thessaly. "They were merely a bunch of homeless nomads, roaming about, attacking and plundering at will. Everything good the Turk is, they learnt it from the Greeks. This is Greek coffee!"

The four-hundred-year-long occupation of Greece by the Ottoman Turks is a very sore point here, understandably. Henry Miller referred to the Turks as "the cruelest enemy a people could have." I pick my arguments about the coffee carefully, but perhaps I should mention that the word "*briki*" is borrowed from the Turkish "*ibrik*", and just leave it at that. Anyway, the Turks got their taste for coffee from the Arabs, according to historians, and the Ottoman Empire spread the drink far and wide. Ron has drunk many a cup brewed over a campfire during his exploits in Arab countries, but it's not his caffeine of choice.

I've never developed a liking for this thick, syrupy coffee whether offered to me in Greece or Turkey or indeed throughout the Balkans, where it's called by a variety of local names, but I am very taken with the pots used to make it. The older pots are usually of copper or brass, but today enamel or stainless steel is more commonly used. Vintage coffee pots can be little works of art. Handmade by craftsmen, they range in style and materials, from the most utilitarian to intricately engraved ones, while some may sport gold or silver decoration on the handle. Even with coffee pots do the affluent make known their status.

"Would you like another cup of tea?" Ron asked as I finished the second one he'd made for me.

"Thanks, now there's at least a chance I might live. That tea was really good. Maybe a bit later."

"Breakfast?"

"Still too early. Let the caffeine work its miracles first," I replied, getting up to walk to the water.

That's when I spotted her. A small woman, clad entirely in black, was trudging along the beach towards us. "Ron," I lowered my voice, "I think she's here."

The short and thickset figure turned into the courtyard with a smile as broad as her face.

"*Kalimera! Kalimera!*" she called out when she saw us.

"*Kalimera,*" I replied. "Good morning."

She was very hot and somewhat breathless. Ron immediately poured her a glass of water and pulled out a chair.

Our first impression of Magda was that she rather resembled an overladen pack mule. She held large carryalls bulging with items in each gnarled hand, and several plastic bags of the grocery store type were hanging over her arthritic wrists. Her pixie-like face was topped by a thick bunch of dark gray curls under which her dark eyes sparkled. In spite of her somewhat disheveled appearance there was a certain dignity about her, and a genuine sweetness.

Magda was delighted that she could speak to me. This was a first in terms of the people her house was rented to.

"*Po! Po! Po!*" she chattered away in great excitement, laughing frequently. "This is wonderful! We can talk together. And your husband is so kind, he is so good, long may he live. May God bless him, but I cannot sit here all day and pretend to be a lady. I must make everything nice for you."

She proceeded to unlock an Aladdin's cave of a storeroom at the side of the house, and bustled about with a plastic tub, buckets, brooms and mops, together with an assortment of cleaning supplies.

"May I go to the bedroom and get the sheets?"

It pained us to see her scrubbing the floors on her knees, washing the sheets and towels outside in the tub, using a bar of soap and a washboard. Magda was well into her seventies at the time; her bent back and swollen limbs testified to a lifetime of hard work. I don't recall if she took any of the hot water from the house – our list of instructions had said to turn the water heater on an hour before we needed it – but at least she had plentiful cold running water and hoses in the garden. Nonetheless, being waited upon by an elderly woman made us feel very uncomfortable.

The sheets were of tightly woven cotton that must have been murder to wring out by hand. Ron insisted on helping her while she protested, but twisting the linens tightly between them certainly got much more of the water out. Magda then pegged everything onto the washing lines, hoisting it all up into the air on bamboo poles where it flapped away in the sunlight and scented breeze. She beamed, well satisfied with her labors. I wondered if she had ever seen a washing machine.

❖ ❖ ❖

The cleaning being completed to her satisfaction, Magda turned her attention to the garden. The area behind the house is very narrow as the hill begins its rapid rise there. There's very little space around her home to establish a garden. In fact, today's regulations would not permit the building of a house so close to the sea. In this limited space chiseled out between the house and the high bank above it, Magda had a number of lemon and orange trees. Protected from the vicious winter seas by the house and from the worst of the winds by the embankment, her trees did well, producing fine fruit. Perhaps they were grateful for the attention she lavished upon them.

Every nook and cranny was either planted with flowers, or contained a pot of flowering plants. Magda loved her flowers, talking to them, cajoling them to bloom, nursing them when they weren't doing well. I believe they were her children for Magda had never borne any. To her great sorrow, and in common with many Greek women of her generation, she was childless. The severe malnutrition suffered by the Greeks during the dreadful war years had profound effects on the development of children. Hundreds of thousands of Greeks died of starvation during the German occupation, far more than from the bombing and other atrocities inflicted upon them in their homeland.

Magda could have taught us a thing or two about recycling. Each of her plant pots had begun its life as a container for something else. Feta cheese and olive oil are among the products one can buy in bulk, supplied in large metal cans. With the tops cut off they make practical planters. Magda had painted some of her large collection with the orange paint commonly used on the wooden fishing boats. She'd obviously done this to stave off the inevitable rusting, but to me the advertising material printed on the canisters was very interesting, especially as some of the manufacturers no longer exist.

Retrieving her plastic bags from the ground where she'd placed them, Magda took up a trowel and set to work. That's when all was revealed - the bags were full of dung! Donkey droppings actually.

"Err, Magda … how do you collect all this?"

"Ah," she beamed at me, "when I walk down to Kalamos."

"You walk to Kalamos? You walk here from Argalasti?" I was incredulous.

"Yes, yes of course. How would I get here otherwise? I have no donkey now."

Ron, sensing that some sort of important conversation was in progress, began to prepare tea and coffee.

"Wait a minute, Magda. Are you seriously telling me you walk all the way down to Kalamos, and then you do the work here? This heavy work?"

She seemed puzzled at my reaction.

"I walk on the *kalderimi*," she replied as though this explained everything. A kalderimi is an age-old cobbled footpath where a donkey and cart could be led. As with the briki discussion, the root of the word is claimed by both Greek and Turk, but one should bear in mind that a large part of what is now Turkey was in fact inhabited by Greeks long before any Turkish state existed. It is often said that if you want to see Greek ruins you should travel to Turkey. The Republic of Turkey only came into existence in 1923, after all the customary disputes and wrangles about territory that follow wars.

The *kalderimi* linking Argalasti and Kalamos is one of the many that crisscross the area. Like all timeworn routes a *kalderimi* generally follows the most accessible course, even if it's not necessarily the shortest.

"So, Magda, how long does it take you to walk down here to Kalamos?"

"About an hour. I pick this up," she indicated the donkey dollops, "along the way. It's very good for the plants."

"Holy cow, Ron," I said as he carried coffee, tea and water out to the courtyard table, "let me tell you this. I can't believe she walks here." I explained what Magda had told me.

"Well, it will certainly be shorter than going by road, I should imagine. It will probably go more or less directly up the hill. Cuts out all the twists and turns."

"Ron, we can't let her walk back. We just can't."

"I agree. Explain to her that when she's finished sharing out the turds we'll take her back."

Magda and I continued chatting as she tended her garden. When she was done she carefully folded up the empty plastic bags and stored them in her tote bag - collecting donkey droppings was evidently an ongoing activity. I admit I was relieved to note that she washed her hands, though I shouldn't have been surprised for Magda was immaculately clean and tidy.

It was past noon by this time. "What do we do, Ron, is she going to stay all afternoon?"

"Look, she's taking the stuff off the line."

Magda was expertly folding the sheets, by now perfectly dried by sun and wind, and putting them into one of her capacious bags.

"Shouldn't the sheets be going back on the bed, Ron? What's she doing?"

"I'm not sure, but she's taking the towels inside."

"Maybe I should I ask her … do you think? She can't be leaving us without sheets, can she?"

Magda bustled out of the house into the courtyard. I sat at the table with my knitting, not knowing how to tackle the problem of what was surely a naked bed.

"I'm finished," she announced. "The bed is changed, the towels are in the bathroom, the house is clean."

"Thank you very much," was my lame reply.

Magda asked to see my knitting and while we were discussing differences in technique, I noticed Ron go into the house. Magda took my work to demonstrate how the yarn is tensioned around the neck in the eastern manner of knitting, her battered hands flying in practiced fashion along the needles.

"It's such a comfort and a joy to make things," she smiled at me. "What would we women do if we didn't have this pleasure?"

Out the corner of my eye I saw Ron emerge from the house, beaming, and holding two thumbs up.

"Not to worry, all's well. Tell Magda we'll take her home."

Puzzled, I did so, but Magda shook her head.

"*Ochi, ochi, ochi.* No, no, no."

I insisted. She protested.

"You are on holiday. You are my guests. It's not for you to take care of me."

We managed to win that argument, and soon the three of us picked our way along to the car to begin negotiating the corkscrew bends to Argalasti.

Once we had deposited Magda safely in the *plateia*, the deserted town square of Argalasti for it was by then the afternoon rest time, Ron explained the mystery of the sheets.

"When I went into the bedroom, the bed was fully made up. She obviously takes the washed sheets back with her to iron, maybe even to finish drying them, and brings the fresh ones with her each time. That's why she had so many bags. She probably also carries extra towels in case the used ones aren't fully dry by the time she leaves."

That figured, and we were to discover that the widowed Magda, elderly, impoverished, alone and God-fearing, was a delightful and most pragmatic character.

TREKKING THE KALDERIMI

"Maybe," said Ron the next day, "we should go hike the *kalderimi* Magda uses. We can have lunch in Argalasti."

"Sounds like a plan. Just let me sort out my knitting." We'd already quizzed Vageli and Eleftheria on it so we knew where to begin the walk.

"I'll take a backpack and you can put your stuff in it. You needn't carry anything."

So off we went, yarn in my pocket, knitting in hand, bottles of water on Ron's back and, I noticed with amusement, the compass keyring hanging from one of the zipper pulls.

To reach the *kalderimi* we needed to turn away from the sea at Bakaloni's and walk along the track we'd driven down, then across the river to Panagia. The tiny church of Panagia stands at one of the springs which provided sweet water to those who dwelt there through the ages. The cobbled path runs right in front of the church, and here we began the hike up to Argalasti, refreshed after letting the cool water run over our hands.

"Ye gods, ancient and otherwise!" I exclaimed when we'd been walking about ten minutes. "This is quite a trek. How on earth does Magda do it after all that work? At her age?"

Kalamos is at the sea, directly on it. Argalasti is 250 meters, some 800-plus feet above sea level. The difference in height is such that Argalasti gets snow in winter, some years enough of it to make life difficult, while snow in Kalamos is a rarity. The kalderimi is steep. It's a lovely hike along the tightly packed stones but not without challenges. The cobbles can be very slick, while the dense vegetation narrows the path considerably in places. If you are lucky, very lucky, you might see a tortoise, but these are disappearing tragically fast because of human intervention. For the birds, the trees and indigenous vegetation are a paradise. They twitter and trill almost incessantly, changing to alarm calls if a hiker might venture too close to a nest.

"But the snakes! How can you walk in these places?" you occasionally hear from those who know little about snakes. The fact is that snakes like you even less than you might like them, hastening away as soon as they feel the vibrations made by the approach of possible danger.

"Ron, hang on. Stop a minute. I need to put my knitting in the backpack."

Too many brambles poked inquisitive fingers out at us for me to risk snagging the work, even though I'm usually able to knit as I walk along. The brief break also gave me an opportunity to catch my breath.

"At least the waddle back will be easier," I opined, but Ron disagreed.

"Not necessarily. On this type of path … steep, and you've got to avoid the branches, it's easy to stumble down the slope. Hard to keep your balance."

Oh joy. So now I could fret about a possible fall. At the very least a broken wrist. That would put paid to the book deadline. My imagination raced ahead.

"Do they have rescue helicopters here? Ron? Ron, do they?"

"I expect so," came the reply from further up the path. "They'll probably have to bring one in from Athens. Why, do you think we'll need one?"

I didn't answer.

"Mind you, how will we call for help?" he added. "There's no signal here for the cell phone, and even if there was what number do we call?"

Another depressing thought. I concentrated on where I was putting my feet.

Suddenly we emerged from the forest to find ourselves at the outskirts of Argalasti from where we could see the gulf, blue and silent, below. Kalamos was a small grouping of specks.

"Wow! What a view! Will you look at that!" said Ron, taking out his camera.

"Hmmm," I perched on a convenient rock to stare down at it all.

The *kalderimi* ended, or began, depending on your direction of travel, at a narrow lane that brought you through to the main square. We discovered later that we'd walked right past Magda's Argalasti home on our way there. We found a taverna where we ate, drank, gathered our wits and prepared to walk back.

"This seemed a good idea at the time," I could have been heard to mutter if there'd been anyone around to hear me.

The downhill run was pretty much as Ron had predicted, so I abandoned any thought of knitting. I'd have dropped a great many stitches if I'd known what Costa, a frequent user of the *kalderimi*, told me some years later. On one memorable occasion as he hurried down the cobbles in the rain, he was met by a wild boar. An absolutely enormous boar possessed of an impressive set of tusks, at least to hear Costa tell it. The poor man spent some considerable time in the embrace of a tree he'd scrambled up, while the great hairy beast, so graphically depicted on ancient Greek pottery and mosaics, waited, showing no desire to leave.

But I didn't know of that encounter then, and now that I've seen my fair share of boar I greatly sympathize with Costa. We made it back to Kalamos with no sign of snake, boar or even donkey droppings, where we napped away the rest of the afternoon.

THE MONASTERY AT PAOU

"You know, Ron," I took a mouthful of my tea the next morning, "you make a really good cuppa. I needed that." We weren't exactly brimming with energy after tramping the *kalderimi*. "How on earth does Magda do it? And carrying all that stuff! Maybe we should have a quieter day today?"

"I can drive us somewhere for lunch, if you like?"

"Thanks. Could be a plan," I nodded, "but let's not rush. I've discovered muscles I didn't know I had, and everyone of them's complaining."

" That *kalderimi* walk is more of a trail hike, Cathy. It's rough. It's not just the gradient, it's also the rocks and holes, pushing branches out of the way… it's very easy to trip. You're not used to it. You could easily have fallen."

We sat in the courtyard, the sea, a deep blue piece of glass, whispering as if unwilling to disturb the peace. The gulls had no such reservations though, screeching their way though the raucous repertoire they've acquired through the millennia.

"Cathy … would you rather stay here today? No problem. We don't have to go anywhere."

"No, true, but we should try to see a bit more. I don't want to go back and feel I've missed something."

"Well, first off there is absolutely no way we can ever see everything, but don't think of this as being the last time we'll ever come here. We'll come back some day. I really like it here."

"Yes, I think we will. Don't know when, but we'll come again. Today, though, maybe let's just go look at this monastery. Here," I held the guide booklet out to Ron, "we see Paou on that road sign where we turn off to Argalasti. It's not far."

"I've got a few emails to write and send off, and when I'm back from the email tree we can go take a look at that monastery. Have you any to send?"

"Yes, but later. My editor needs some stuff about the book. Anyway, they're asleep now – I'll do it after lunch."

We cleared away our breakfast things and tidied up, though there was very little to do. Ron took the phone and the computer and set off up the hill. I watched two gulls in vicious argument over something one of them had plucked from the water, the victor finally flying away with what looked like a piece of seaweed. The loser retreated to a rock, muttering to any passing gull that might have been inclined to listen.

Later that morning we set off along the beach from Magda's, stopping to chat a bit to *kyria* Katina who was sitting alone at her usual spot outside on the promenade with her crochet work and a coffee.

"He's gone to Volos," she told us, "to get supplies."

"We should go to Volos too," I climbed into the car, "I'd like to look around a bit ... see the buildings, what sort of stuff's in the stores. Is there a knitting shop? Maybe next week sometime."

"Volos definitely. Centuries of history there. Jason and the Argonauts myth for starters. It was based on something – many set sail from that harbor searching for gold, for something better in their lives. They panned the rivers, using a sheepskin, and the gold dust would settle in it."

We crossed the bridge and drove along the seafront. The very narrow road, separated from the water's edge by a few feet of sandy beach, makes for some interesting negotiations when two vehicles approach each other. At the far end of the beach the road takes a sharp left turn and you wend your uphill way along to a T-junction at the very top. A lopsided road sign points to Argalasti on the left, and to Paou on the right.

A flock of sheep was grazing in the fields as we drove past, their vigilant sheepdogs watching us. Almost all the sheep were white but a couple of black ones among them, together with the classic black and white of the dogs, made for an interesting study in black and white. Dense areas of dark green scrubland accentuated how brown the grasslands had become after the long, dry summer, while the shepherd, almost hidden in the shade at the edge of the bushes, caught my eye with a flash of vivid red. Ah, a shepherdess in a red blouse. Not quite the romanticized pastoral scene beloved by European artists of the past, but nonetheless a very pleasant picture of everyday life in a farming community.

As we approached the monastery, I saw why the shepherdess had chosen to feed her flock there that day. Probably one of reasons that the monks had built their Byzantine complex of church and cloister there in the late 1700s. Water. Water in abundance. Pure water from a spring.

The sheep had no concern for the location, but the monks most surely did. The monastery at Paou was established atop a cliff which commands spectacular views of the gulf and the several small islands in its waters. The site is awe-inspiring. It sent shivers down my spine. I knew, I just somehow knew that the spot wasn't an accidental choice. This was no random decision by the abbot or the church leader at the time. Here something had already existed. Something of significance. Thessaly's Neolithic history is considerable, the subject of continuous study, attracting archaeologists and scholars from prestigious institutions. Evidence continues to be uncovered of even earlier human occupation during the Paleolithic period. Simply put, Thessaly's story is one buried deep in the very ancient past.

There are caves in the cliffs below the monastery, with proof of habitation from prehistory. Hunter-gatherers would have had food in abundance, from land and from sea. Millennia passed. Man became more sophisticated. Creation myths led to worship of the Olympian gods, and what more impressive locale for an early temple than the area now known as Paou? It likely has a narrative like that of Bath Abbey, with its Neolithic history of the Somerset region, the ancient well, the temples.

We parked the Elantra near some ruined stone buildings of much more modern vintage. They appeared to have been used as animal pens, but perhaps they date from the days of the monastery and were accommodations of some sort, maybe for workers not part of the monastic community. The entrance to the monastery compound is lined with imposing cypress trees. Hard to tell their age for the cypress is long-lived, and a symbol of immortality since at least the Classical era, sacred to the Greek goddess Artemis and her twin, Apollo.

The vista through the trees can only be described as breathtaking. A cliché, yes, but that's exactly the effect it has on one. The waters of the Pagasitic lay below, the islands rising like enormous mounds of emeralds from its depths, tossed there by some gigantic hand. No boat marked the water. The air was still, the ceaseless drone of insects all that could be heard. We didn't speak. We stood. We stared. We pondered.

I broke the silence. "There are no words." And indeed at that moment there weren't. It was as if all Nature had come together to present her work and the work of human hands in one instant to be carved forever into memory.

We walked on to the entrance gate in the stone wall surrounding the courtyard. The monastery, dedicated to Saint Nicholas, had been partly destroyed by the Turks during their occupation of Thessaly, and was rebuilt. I presume it was done so more or less along the original lines. Perhaps enough of it remained that reconstructing the walls was relatively straightforward, or maybe there were some drawings available in the archives that would have helped. The lovely chapel - the focal point of the monks' devotions - had suffered great damage. The eyes of the Christ, the Virgin Mary and the saints which are such an integral part of Byzantine art had been shot out, and the rest of the paintings peppered with bullet holes. This disfiguring is characteristic of the desecration inflicted on icons and religious art during the Ottoman occupation of Greece. The Paou frescoes have been restored since we first saw them and much as I appreciate the painstaking work of the artist, they're nevertheless a reminder of the senseless and deliberate destruction carried out the world over during times of upheaval, by vandals and thugs of every ilk.

The monks' cells formed part of the monastery's outer walls so that the compound could be secured against enemy forces, though it wasn't able to withstand the attack of 1843. How terrible that must have been for the monks. How traumatic to witness the sacrilegious storming of the chapel, the very embodiment of their faith.

IN THE MONASTERY GARDEN

I left the inner courtyard, and began exploring the grounds below the building with their outlook over the Gulf, the mainland stretching away into central Greece, no dust or cloud to interrupt the continuity. The olive groves, planted in meticulous rows, were extensive but in great need of pruning. Those trees were standing in silent witness to the havoc when the Turks came.

Darker foliage began to appear amongst the silvery greens of the olives and I found myself in what was once a well-tended orchard. Orange and lemon trees bore some ripening fruits among dark green leaves; scattered around them on the ground among the weeds lay miniature oranges and lemons which hadn't survived the neglect.

A large vineyard was staked out on the slopes below the citrus, but it too was much in need of attention. The vines were thick and sturdy. They'd been there a long time. They had a perfect position above the sea, well drained, facing the sun through long, hot days, but they had not seen loving care for a considerable period. I could hear Ron walking towards me. "Come see these sad grapevines, Ron. Look," I picked up a pathetic dried-out remnant of a bunch of grapes and held it out to him, "this must have been here for years."

"You know," he examined the vines, "I'm no expert but I think these have been attended to at times. These haven't been completely abandoned since the Turks left. Locals probably tried to keep cultivating at least some of the stuff here … but what with the wars and all the other things people had to contend with … well, it surely wasn't easy."

"Can't you just see the monks stomping the grapes, though," I laughed. "I bet they took the greatest care of these. Those locked-up buildings back there probably have huge wine casks in them. Well, they must have had a good life until it was all destroyed." I wasn't going to think about what the fate of the monks might have been once the Turks arrived.

"I'll look around a bit more, Cathy. This was a sizeable garden at one time. The monks must have been quite self sufficient."

"Yes, but then everybody had to be. If you didn't grow it, forage for it or kill it, then you'd have a miserable life, I imagine. But look, over there. I think those are artichoke plants. I'm going to see if that was a veggie garden."

There was a great deal of undergrowth that might have been some sort of cultivated plants in the past but, apart from the artichokes and a mass of rosemary which had grown into great unruly hedges, I couldn't identify much of anything. The unmistakable cyclamen had begun to showcase their dainty flowers - little pink blooms were poking up from the variegated leaves. Clustered on the ground cyclamen grow low, their flowers immediately catching the eye. Here in this overgrown orchard, protected from the heat and blazing sun, they were able to appear earlier than those on the fields.

Raising my eyes from the cyclamen I noticed the distinctive fruit of the pomegranate tree in a little grove. I'd never seen the fruit growing on the tree. I knew it only in wooden crates in supermarkets, nestling among straw. Weeds abounded in the stony ground, catching at my feet as I made my way over to the trees for a closer look, dislodging a grasshopper or two in the process.

The trees were tall and many-branched, quite dense; they'd been there a great many years. The branches were thick with pomegranates in various stages of ripening, their hexagonal sides streaked with crimson, deepest pink, gold and yellow. Each looked like a miniature setting sun peeping out from behind bunches of dark green leaves. I stood under the trees, gazing out at the almost blinding blue and turquoise of the Gulf, trying to recall what I knew of the pomegranate in Greek mythology. Something to do with winter, I vaguely remembered, and Persephone. Lost in my reverie I reached up to touch a shiny red and pink pomegranate hanging just in front of me, and froze. A couple of inches from my face, protruding from the branches, was the unmistakable slender head and eye of a snake. A greenish-colored snake. A snake draped in a tree. Having grown up in Africa I am well acquainted with the *boomslang,* which means tree snake in Afrikaans and which can kill you. In all fairness it's not generally aggressive and death from it is rare, providing you receive immediate treatment. Still, a boomslang is not high on most people's lists for an intimate encounter.

The snake and I stared at each other. Transfixed, I didn't dare move. "Ron," I finally managed to squeak. "Ron, a snake. Come. Please." I had no time to consider my options for Ron had heard me and summed up the situation immediately.

"I'm here on your left," he murmured, so as not to alarm me further for snakes have no ears and are alerted only by movement and vibration. "I'm going to count to three, and then you throw out your left arm and I'll grab you."

I did and he did, yanking me hard from the tree as the snake flashed away through the branches, rustling the leaves in a spine-chilling wave of coils. He was a big fella.

"Ron, what kind of snake was he? You any idea? He couldn't have been a boomslang, right?"

"We can ask, Cathy, or look it up somewhere. But no, he'll be indigenous to the area. Are you alright?

"Yes, but I would like to know what he is. I'd also like to check up on Persephone. You know, the myth?"

"Can't say that I remember it, but I've brought a copy of Edith Hamilton with me. We can look it up at Magda's."

We had no Google in those days, but Ron had as usual saved the day. I was anxious to get back to the house and read what Hamilton, that great classicist and expert on Greek mythology, had to say about Persephone.

BACK AT BAKALONI'S

We wandered around the deserted monastery grounds for a while, finally returning to Kalamos. This time both Bakalonis were sitting outside and Bakaloni immediately poured Ron an ouzo.

"How was it in Volos?" I continued knitting while Bakaloni recounted his frustration with the traffic, the price of goods from the wholesalers, the hurried attitude of the *Voliotes* – the residents of Volos – who had too many airs and graces, and why he preferred the quiet life of the Pelion Peninsula. *Kyria* Katina, who could probably have recited his peevish litany from memory, said nothing. Putting out her hand to examine my knitting, she noted that I was working on a different piece. I nodded. No point in trying again to explain the deadline I was committed to. Life moved at a very different pace there alongside the sea. I loved it.

"So, where did you go this morning?" *kyria* Katina asked. "Ah yes, the monastery. People go there for their water. It's very pure water. From deep in the ground."

I commented that the area around the monastery would have had a long history, a history reaching back well before the birth of Christ, and that there might well have been a temple to one of the Greek gods even then. She didn't appear too keen to discuss that, saying that the Ancients had indeed been in Pelion, but they were not Christians. That seemed rather dismissive to me, but there was no point in pursuing that debate. Instead I asked what fresh fruit they had for sale.

"Nothing now," Bakaloni told me, "because tomorrow is the market and everybody will buy from there."

"What market? Where is it?"

"In Argalasti. Every Saturday in Argalasti. In the center. You should go there early," *kyria* Katina answered. "It's a very popular market. For the people. You can buy a lot of things there. Clothes too. Even knitwear."

I explained to Ron, and then told her that we would definitely go. "Is there anything I can get for you?"

She shook her head and thanked me, saying they had everything they needed. We got up to leave. Ron bought a bottle of milk and a loaf of bread.

"For your poor starving sea gulls," he teased me. I tore bits off the bread for the gulls as we walked the short stretch back to Magda's.

"I wonder if there's any myth about seagulls, Ron? You'd think there would be, but I don't recall one."

"I do remember something vaguely. They were minor gods, gods of the sea. You can look it up in Hamilton's book. I'll fetch it for you."

"Thanks, but I'm more interested in getting the story of Persephone sorted out right now."

The afternoon passed pleasantly in Magda's courtyard. The boats swayed about in the water in front of us, while even the gulls took a break from their perpetual shrieks of indignation. Ron worked in his notebook on a physics problem, and I read Hamilton.

"Ron, what do you remember about Persephone and the pomegranate?"

"Didn't she pull an Eve on the crowd?"

"What do you mean?"

"Well, didn't she eat a pomegranate that she wasn't supposed to? And then she was sent away. Something like that, I think."

"Yes, the ancient Greeks had quite an involved tale about her that explained winter and summer. Her mother was Demeter. She was the goddess of harvests, so she was pretty much connected to summer. She was very protective of Persephone who was apparently both beautiful and good, and then one day Persephone was out picking wildflowers …"

"That's right, Cathy, yes, I remember now, and then Hades snuck up from his Underworld and kidnapped her."

"As I was saying, Ron, poor Demeter was mad with grief at her daughter's disappearance and she asked the gods for help. Anyway, long story short, Hades was ordered to let her go and he tricked her into eating some pomegranate seeds, and that meant she had to go back to him for part of every year. Hence winter and summer."

"Right. Winter was when she had to leave Demeter on earth and return to the Underworld. And then nothing grew because of Demeter's grief which made the earth dark and cold."

"It's funny, Ron, that you mentioned Eve, because some sources say that it was a pomegranate that Eve ate, and not an apple."

"Pomegranate, apple ... got them both into trouble, didn't it? That's women for you."

I threw a peach pit at him.

TO MARKET, TO MARKET …

"Another cup of tea?"

"No thanks. Ron, when do you think we should go up to this market?"

It was not yet 7.00 am but already there was activity on the water in front of us. A dinghy that had been lying on the beach through the week was being rowed out to a large boat at anchor in deeper water; two men carrying fishing gear were wading to a small *caïque*.

"It's the weekend. Saturday. Seems like people come down to their beach houses. They've got nice weather for it."

"Yes, it's a lovely day, at least so far. Ron, maybe *kyria* Katina is right and we should go up early to the market. Could be these weekenders will get supplies there."

'Depends what they're looking for, and also depends on what's being sold. I don't think there'll be more than basic essentials there, Cathy. I can't see antiques and such for sale there."

"Well, she said all kinds of things get sold. Let's get a move on and have breakfast. I want to go. There may be some textiles … good pickings perhaps … but not if the dealers get there first."

We tidied up, locked the house and began walking to the car. *Kyria* Katina was sweeping in front of the little shop, a mop sticking out of her apron pocket, while Bakaloni arranged the tables and chairs. We exchanged greetings, remarking on the glorious weather which they told me was often perfect at that time of very late summer. Yes, I confirmed that we were going to the market and with their kind wishes for a good day, we drove off.

Argalasti on a weekday and Argalasti on Saturday made their differences abundantly clear as we turned onto the main road, leaving the last view of the Gulf behind us at that point. Traffic was heavy. In a manner of speaking, of course, for heavy traffic in those days meant that a driver needed to wait a minute or so to break into the flow of vehicles.

"Are they all going to the market do you think?"

"Probably," said Ron, "certainly they're going into Argalasti."

"*To market, to market, to buy a fat pig!*" I sang out. "Sorry, just popped into my head from childhood."

"Pigs? Did *kyria* Katina tell you it was a livestock market?"

"Gosh, I hope not! No, it can't be. It's just going to be fresh produce, surely? Farm goods. She did mention clothes though."

Traffic had slowed down as we approached the crossroads in the center of Argalasti, almost to a crawl.

"Looks like we'll have a parking problem. There's no empty spot I can see."

We'd always parked in front of the church, by the bus stop, when we'd gone to buy groceries. This time cars and vans were parked and stopped in a multi-colored jumble through which people pushed in every direction. Mothers with kids, kids with bikes, ladies with wheeled shopping trolleys, mothers with all the above. Tiny old ladies, invariably dressed in black, made their often painful way along with a basket in one hand, a walking stick in the other. All was cheerful confusion. At least it was to the uninitiated, the newbies in town, but after a few minutes while Ron tried to navigate to a parking spot, it all suddenly fell into place. Like a kaleidoscope the pattern emerged: what vehicles were settled in for a while and which were merely dropping people off; that pickup on the corner was selling fish; those taxis parked opposite the church were waiting to drive customers home with their goods; that battered truck in front of the filling station was stacked high with clay pots, while next to it stood an elderly man selling balloons.

Ron finally squeezed into a spot between two rather battered cars and we climbed cautiously out.

"These look like the Fiat I had hundreds of years ago, Ron. What are they?"

"They're Russian-made and yes, they're based on the Fiat 124. They're called Lada. Very popular. I saw a lot when I was in Moscow. Quite cheap and fairly reliable."

"Awful colors though, Ron. My Fiat was a gorgeous blue."

"Well, if you don't offer many colors you can keep the costs down. Ford apparently said you could have his Model T car in any color so long as it was black."

People were walking up the road leading away from the crossroads. We followed like sheep. I could see heaps of empty fruit crates cast to the side of the street, canvas awnings propped up on poles over some of the stalls, most of them piled high with goods, and eager sellers assuring potential customers of the quality of their products.

"Nowhere, lady, will you see such sheets and towels as I can offer you!"

"But my prices are far better than his. Come and see for yourself!"

"Here, taste this plum! Does it not melt in your mouth? Or this peach!"

The noise was incessant, but not unpleasant. It was the sound of activity, of human interaction, of banter and conversation and a great deal of good-natured haggling.

My eye was drawn to a display of textiles. Hand-embroidered pillowcases with crocheted flounces, cushion covers and table runners done in various kinds of handwork, tablecloths of all sizes, handwoven coverlets and rugs, and exquisite baby items. The seller, an attractive woman wearing a dainty crocheted blouse, noticed how carefully I was studying an embroidered pillowcase, and spoke to me in English. I answered in Greek and she beamed at me even more.

We discussed the item.

"*Kyria*, I see you understand expert work."

"Yes, indeed. I can't believe how perfect this embroidery is," I enthused. "I can't tell the right side from the wrong side. It's fabulous. Who does this kind of work?"

She explained that her source was an accomplished needlewoman. "She lives high on the mountains of the north, near Ioannina. She loves to do this work. She has done it since a small child."

We chatted away until another customer needed her attention, and after she'd attended to her and a sale had been concluded, I asked how she obtained the goods from her supplier.

"I have family in that area, so every three months or so I go to visit them and I see this lady then. Her name is Maria. She usually has quite a few pieces for me, but …" she tailed off.

"What do you mean?" though I had a horrible feeling that I already knew. "She's getting old, is that it?"

"Yes, and I don't know how long she will continue."

I selected several pieces, including all the baby clothes as these are always very useful to keep on hand for gifts.

The vendor listed the items in a receipt book and handed me a copy.

Ron was ready with the money. He'd seen my eyes glaze over! I am no mathematician, and what seemed vast amounts in Greek drachma would begin to panic me.

We thanked the good lady and moved off, me clutching my treasures.

"Don't get worked up over the drachs, Cathy. It sounds confusing but it isn't really. You can easily work it out if you know the exchange rate. You paid just over thirty dollars for your stuff. Not bad at all."

No, indeed it wasn't. We wandered around the various stalls. The clothing on offer didn't appeal much to me, but some interesting leather pieces on a small table did. The trader was an African man. I noticed how polite he was, and how he made a considerable effort to speak to a possible customer in Greek.

"*Kalimera, kyria*," he addressed me.

"Good morning," I replied in English, "we're both a long way from home."

We had a friendly conversation. He'd been in Greece for several years he told me, but didn't explain how that had come about and I didn't like to ask. He was clean-shaven, wearing jeans and a crisp white shirt. His cheeks and forehead bore the tribal scarifications which would identify him in his home country as being of a particular tribe.

Unwilling to question him directly, I said: "I can tell you are not Zulu. The Zulu I grew up among marked their faces very differently."

"Yes, madam, you are quite right. I am Nigerian. I am Yoruba. In some parts of my country now this cutting is no longer allowed, but I am proud to be Yoruba. We are changing too much in my country. We are losing our culture."

I merely nodded. What should I have said? Should I have asked why he was no longer in Nigeria? I didn't feel it my place to do so. He must have had the papers he needed in order to be in Greece, or he wouldn't have been able to trade in the market. For this a license is required.

Ron picked out a leather belt. I selected two wallets. We exchanged good wishes as we left to choose fruit and vegetables. That proud Yoruban man whose culture existed millennia before the time of Christ, has stayed in my mind ever since. Whatever the reason that he, like the countless many before and after him, was no longer living in the country of his birth, I hope that his life is a good one.

"Right, that's all put away then. Do you want to go to the bakery or something?" Ron shut the car door after he'd loaded our purchases.

We'd worked our way through the growing crowds back to the car. *Kyria* Katina was right – one needed to go early. For many of the folk on the Peninsula, especially the elderly, Argalasti was the only place they shopped for groceries and other essentials. The Saturday market provides clothing, shoes, bath towels, sheets and other household textiles, rugs, kitchenware and a great many other useful and necessary items, in addition to fruit and veg, free range eggs, plants. And honey. The most delicious honey. Honey from bees which range all over the Pelion Peninsula, infusing the thick golden food they make with flavors from the profusion of wild plants found from the mountain to the sea.

"Yes, let's get some bread. No, stop making faces! Not just for the gulls, I give them white bread anyway, but some wholegrain bread to eat with the honey we bought."

We were in luck. Because we'd gone in to Argalasti early there were still a few loaves of the most delicious and nutritious whole grain bread left. I bought a selection of cookies to give to *kyria* Katina. These are sold by the weight, and packaged in a cardboard box, tied with ribbon. They look so festive. While I was at it I got some for us too, and left Ron to handle the drachma involved.

HOME AGAIN, HOME AGAIN …

We retrieved the Elantra, and drove back to the turnoff for Paou/Kalamos. Once we left the main road the traffic immediately lessened. The view down to Kalamos stunned us. Again. No other word can describe it for it takes your breath away. An amphitheater lies before you, the mountains and hills rising up like tiered seating from the sea. On that day of the most wonderful weather, the performers on the deep blue stage were the boats. Small boats, almost all of them white, and white-sailed yachts, reminiscent of the actors in ancient Greek theater.

We reached the beachfront of Kalamos where a complete contrast to the weekday scene presented itself. Although the summer was fading away into nostalgic memory there were still quite a few vacationers in Pelion, but locals with children back in school came at the weekends to enjoy the beach. And then only if the approaching autumnal weather played nice. Everyone and their mother was there that Saturday. Everyone seemed to be having a good time. As for the kiddies who had recently been herded back into the classroom, the freedom was intoxicating.

We crossed the bridge over to our side of Kalamos. The quieter side, with the little harbor right in front of Magda's. We parked the car so as not to annoy She-of-the-Parking-Authority, gathered up our purchases and walked across to the Bakalonis. Busy! They were really busy, serving coffee, cold drinks, ouzo and snacks to relaxed and happy customers. Hyper-excited children were racing about on the little promenade, chasing each other, jumping in and out of the water, squealing and shrieking in delight, with the occasional tears and wails that invariably accompany a commotion of kids. *Kyria* Katina was in the kitchen. I popped in to give her the cookies and said I'd see her later. She already looked exhausted.

"*Home again, home again, jiggety-jig!*" said Ron as we put our bags down on the courtyard table.

I laughed and went inside to sort out our shopping. "So, we're going to have a very healthy lunch, Ron. A Greek salad, this fabulous bread – we can have it with cheese - and there's still a few slices of ham. But I can't wait to have it with honey."

"What about some of this vino collapso?" Ron took the bottle out of the fridge. Or would you rather have tea?"

"I'll stick to tea. I've got knitting instructions to write up this afternoon … I'd better not get muddled."

We wiped down the table, arranged our foodstuffs and settled in for a leisurely meal as we watched the boats and the gulls on the water.

"I'll have a couple more of those very healthy cookies, Ron. The choccy ones. Don't look at me like that! The cocoa bean is a vegetable, right? No, maybe it's a fruit, or is it a seed? Whatever … it's good for my soul."

❖ ❖ ❖

We dined at Vageli's that night. So did half the population of Kalamos, it appeared. Saturday night at Galini's taverna was the place to be, and most deservedly. Why seek a meal elsewhere when Eleftheria prepared food more than worthy of the gods? They had their ambrosia up there on Mt. Olympus, but did they have *loulouthakia*? Did they feast on lamb *stifado*? If they dined on chicken, slowly and succulently braised with onions and prunes, infused with herbs and spices blended with a skillful hand, I'm unaware of it. This was the banquet we devoured, together with a wonderful array of meze, picking morsels from each other's plates, and not holding back on the wine. The lamb with pearl onions and tomatoes melted in the mouth, the chicken teased the palate as we tried to identify the seasonings, but it was the *loulouthakia* that I fell completely, hopelessly in love with. Stuffed zucchini blossoms. Little flowers is exactly what they are, for the word means just that - little flowers. Eleftheria's little flowers are memorable. I have never found their equal.

Eleftheria and Vageli were run off their feet, so we didn't linger for conversation would have been impossible. We raved about the food, Ron counted out the drachmas, we nodded here and there to folk who greeted us and left, promising to return soon. We tottered our very happy way back to Magda's, but only because the ground was uneven and the sandy beach kept on putting rocks in our way. I even forgot to scan the path for scorpions.

OF STOREROOMS AND OLIVES

"Magda's coming tomorrow, right?"

"So she said, but I'm not going to let her do a lot of cleaning, Ron. We've hardly dirtied the place and she must get very tired."

"Yes. I was thinking that way she would finish early and we could drop her in Argalasti and then drive around a bit. See something of those places you've been telling me about. We can grab a meal somewhere."

Magda arrived the next morning as promised. She was hot, and quite breathless, but beaming as she walked into the little courtyard and dropped her assortment of bags on the ground. "*Kalimera! Kalimera! Ti kanete?*"

"Good morning! Good morning! How are you?"

She threw her arms around me, then drew back, still hugging me, to study my face. "Are you having a good time? Is there anything I can do for you?"

Bless her heart. Ron guided her into a chair and poured her a glass of water. "*Kafe*?"

Magda shook her head. "*Ochi, efcharisto*." No, thank you.

"He must not worry about me," she told me. "It's not for him to look after me. But he is a really lovely man. Tell him he's a very good man."

"Yes, please Ron, she says no but she really needs some coffee. I'll get her some of those cookies we bought."

Ron busied himself in the kitchen while I chatted with Magda. I didn't have the heart to tell her that I'd appointed him tea and coffee maker because the gas affair frankly terrified me, though it was a perfectly good appliance.

"Magda, in those bags – have you brought clean sheets?"

"Yes, yes, of course. Is there a problem?" She began to rise from the chair.

"No, no, sit," I eased her back down. "Ron and I will take the sheets from the beds, and if you'll give me the clean ones, we'll change them. Then you can wash the others at home in Argalasti. That will be easier for you."

Magda began protesting.

"What's going on, Cathy? Is she upset about something?"

"No, I'm just telling her to give us the sheets – she has fresh sheets with her – and we'll do it."

"Good plan." Ron went inside and soon emerged with the sheets neatly folded. "There. I've stripped the beds. Ask her to give me the clean ones. She can put these in her bag."

Magda's face was a picture! She clucked and fussed and repeatedly apologized .

"But why, Magda? Why can't we help you a little? It's not a problem at all. Sit."

But she wouldn't sit, and soon all three of us were in the bedroom, Ron and I making up the beds, with Magda wielding a broom and duster. She kept up a steady stream of blessings on us, breaking off occasionally to reprimand herself for her perceived failings. Ron couldn't understand her but he caught the inflections in her voice.

"She's quite worked up, isn't she?"

"I think it's because she's not accustomed to talking to the people who stay here."

With the room cleaned and the beds – there were two singles – made up to her satisfaction, we trooped back out to the courtyard again.

Magda had opened the storage buildings alongside the house when she'd retrieved the broom.

"Magda, may I look inside?"

"Of course, of course. Come and see. I'll be back soon."

"Where are you going?"

"To clean the bathroom."

"Oh no, you're not. The bathroom's perfectly clean. This is more important to me. No, I want you to stay here and tell me what all this is." Inside the first building I could see two enormous wooden barrels, about eight feet high, with handmade wooden ladders leaning against them. "These barrels are very interesting. What are they for? Do you still use them? *Ochi* Magda, no, I'm not concerned about the bathroom."

Magda, firm in her belief that cleanliness is next to godliness, followed me with great reluctance into the storeroom. The barrels were huge, tightly banded at close intervals with iron secured by nails. All the metal was very rusted.

"These look like handmade nails." Ron had come in and was examining the barrels. "Yes, see how irregular the nailheads are. Not factory produced, that's for sure. The village blacksmith hammered these out. And quite a long time ago."

"So, Magda, these are old. What were they for?"

"Olives. Here we stored the olives. My husband's family. Yiorgo's family. God rest his soul." She crossed herself.

It was dark inside the building. Magda flicked a switch hanging from a cord fastened high up in the rafters and a dim light came on.

"Very dicey, that. Very dangerous. Don't touch it, Cathy. Be careful how you move around in here."

There was very little room to move, as it happened, for the building was crammed with stuff. It looked to my ignorant eye to be of about the same vintage as the older structures in Panagia. The walls were of rock, with earth and pebbles as the mortar. Great handcut beams spanned the walls, to which were fastened the roof supports. It looked sturdy enough, but given its evident age and the constant possibility of earth tremor, who could really say. The floor was earthen. The odor of mold and damp permeated everything. How could it not given its proximity to the sea?

"Let's go sit outside, Magda. I want you to tell me all about this."

We seated ourselves in the courtyard. Magda answered my questions and I explained to Ron. As far as Magda knew, the storage buildings were at least a hundred and fifty years old, and had been in her late husband's family since they were constructed; the family had long owned the land and the olive groves. Their olive harvests increased and became more profitable, leading to the building of the storerooms. Business prospered. There was so much work that the cottage had been added, enabling the workers to remain on site and make full use of the daylight hours. Convenient. A bit like living above the shop, but what a location the shop had.

I kept glancing back into the storeroom as Magda talked. The harvested olives were cured in those gigantic barrels, an operation which was labor intensive as I understood it from Magda's account. Apparently her husband's relatives had done very well, but they had worked hard for their success.

"So Magda, it wasn't olive oil in those barrels?"

"No, no. That's not the same thing. Here olives were prepared for the table. For sale. To other countries even."

I paid attention as she outlined the production process. "The olives were knocked out of the trees by beaters with long sticks. *Kalámia.* Canes. These grew along the river, and the workers would cut them as they were needed."

The penny dropped. Kalamos! Of course. That's how the village got its name. From the tall, thick reeds which still grow in small patches in Kalamos.

"The olives would fall onto the cloths laid out under the trees. Today it's easy. Now there are these big plastic cloths."

She was referring to tarpaulins. I was fascinated to learn that the best way to gather olives is by hand, but time is valuable, hence the need to beat them off the trees. For centuries cloths for the olive harvest were woven from linen, from cotton, from suitable plant material.

"Everybody worked. All the family worked. The little children too. The olives must be put into baskets. People worked all day. All day."

"So Magda, you worked here? On these lands?"

"No, no, I didn't know my husband then. No, I worked on my own people's trees. I started when I was four years old."

I was fascinated by what she had to tell. Once the olives had been gathered up, they had to be sorted, she explained to us.

"We had long tables and the olives would be spread out and the leaves and bits of stick had to be cleaned out. Also any olives that were damaged. Then they were put into the barrels."

The barrels had water and salt in them, she told me. The right proportion had to be maintained, and the water changed as needed.

"So people climbed up on the ladders and emptied the olives into the barrels," she continued, "and you couldn't delay because the olives got acid after being picked. But my husband's family had a business, a good business."

❖ ❖ ❖

There was so much I wanted to ask her, but I was itching to get back into that olive room to see what else was inside there. And when I did, I wasn't disappointed. Beautiful old olive oil jars stood half buried in the floor. Earthenware amphorae and pitchers for oil, water, wine, together with bowls and platters were stacked against a wall, presumably no longer used. Many bore designs which were either painted on, or incised into the clay. There were pieces of wooden furniture, all hand made, hand carved, some painted with typical folk art motifs. An attractive handwoven bedspread or some kind of coverlet was draped over a table close to the door. From the irregular bulges under it I guessed that it was protecting a variety of items. Perhaps these were things Magda removed from the house so they'd not be damaged by tenants.

Copper cauldrons and various implements were gathered into any available space. The farming tools were very interesting. A pitchfork propped in a corner caught my eye. As far as I could tell in the dim light it had no join in it at all and concluded that it was carved from one log. The handle or shaft was entirely one piece which formed the central prong, with two prongs on either side. That five-pronged instrument was a work of art, carved by whom and when? It belonged in a museum.

Magda seemed surprised at my interest. "Just many old things," she dismissed the items. To her, maybe. I didn't like to ask but perhaps they weren't part of her life with Yiorgo. Given the thick mantle of dust on everything they'd been in there for a good long while and held no memories for anyone anymore. The abundance of spider webs in the entrance area testified to the fact that these close cousins of scorpions pretty much had the run of the place. Suspicious scuttling in the dimness convinced me that I'd seen enough, and I was soon back outside.

"You're not cleaning anything else," I told Magda as she advanced on the kitchen with bucket and mop. Look after your plants. Please. Then we'll go out and take you up to Argalasti."

I sat at the table with my knitting, Ron headed off to the email tree and a rather bewildered Magda applied herself to her plants. With trowel in hand she fed them the droppings from her bags which she then watered in with the hose. I could hear her talking in soft tones to them. Sweet words. Encouraging words. She and Prince Charles. Worlds apart in every possible way, yet joined by a fierce love and respect for that which grows from the earth.

Magda returned her tools to the olive shed.

"Right, we're finished," I told her. "That's it for today. We're taking you home now. We want to drive around and explore a bit more."

She protested, but finally fastened the big doors of the shed together with a hefty padlock. I glanced at Ron, both of us thinking the same thing: that lock would deter nobody, a child could yank it off. Still, it must have given her a measure of reassurance though frankly, I couldn't think of anyone in the area who'd be interested in the goods inside.

We locked the front door of her cottage and walked together back to the car. Our ears ringing with Magda's thanks and blessings, we dropped her off in Argalasti and sat in the car for a moment to consider our options.

A TIGHT SQUEEZE IN LEFOKASTRO

"What about that place you mentioned, Cathy? Something about a castle?"

"Yes, it's along the coast, before you get to Kalamos. It's called Lefokastro. *Kastro* means castle. The name means white castle. You want to go see it?"

"Yes, why not? Could be interesting."

Ron swung left into the main roadway and I scanned the roadside for a signpost. One eventually appeared, proclaiming Lefokastro/Kalamos.

Ron turned into the marked road. "It seems there's another way into Kalamos. Makes sense. If you're coming from Volos there's no reason to drive through Argalasti unless you need to. We might try it later."

Open land flanked the road, allowing a panorama of Mt. Pelion from whose heights water has flowed for aeons into the Pagasitic Gulf lying in front of us.

"Ron, do you think all this … it's pastureland, right … do you think it was always like this? No trees?"

"Probably not. The area is well known for its forests, even in antiquity. No, this looks to have been cleared at some point. There's dense forest in the gullies along the main road. It's much easier to clear forest that's on flat land."

We reached a fork in the road. To the right lay Lefokastro according to a small sign, and straight ahead one could continue to Kalamos.

"That two-humped thing on the sign to Kalamos, Ron, that means a river bed?"

"No, it means it's a bad road. A rough road. It's a dirt track, and quite narrow by the look of it."

The Kalamos road was lower than the surrounding land and had obviously been bulldozed into existence; rather a long time ago, judging by its appearance. The elevated ground at the junction was thick with *maquis* – the indigenous shrubland that grows profusely in the Mediterranean areas if it's left undisturbed. Almost buried in the bush behind the signpost, and with a large tree right in front of it, stood a small, lopsided structure. Most of the roughly applied whitewash had disintegrated so that the concrete blocks of its construction were visible. In keeping with its Greek Orthodox tradition it was topped by a dome, a rather misshapen one under which an opening had been constructed.

"Ah look Ron, it's an *iconostasis*. It's a little shrine. I wonder how old it is? It looks quite neglected."

We stopped for a closer inspection. A cracked glass door set into a metal frame protected an icon of the Virgin Mary inside, a framed image painted on wood. Tucked into the frame was a card with a picture of a saint, but it was too faded for me to identify. There was a bottle of oil and a red glass container with a candle, a box of matches lying next to it. The flame had long been extinguished. The glass door was very dirty, and I couldn't make out any indication of why the shrine had been erected. These are typically dedicated to a particular saint, to Jesus or the Holy Trinity in supplication or in gratitude for a prayer answered. I would have loved to know the history of this extremely simple and heartfelt token of devotion, but I had no idea who to ask about it. I wondered if the person who had erected the *iconostasis* there was perhaps no longer alive. Given that a tree had grown tall right in front of it, partly blocking any access to it, that little shrine had been built some considerable time ago.

◈ ◈ ◈

In fields to our right a large flock of sheep was grazing. The shepherd appeared to be taking a nap under a small tree, perhaps drowsy from the heat for although the sun, Helios, had begun his journey to bring longer days to the southern hemisphere, it was still very warm. The gorgeous black and white sheepdogs were ever-vigilant in guarding the sheep, raising their heads to track us as we drove by. These magnificent dogs have an ancient history in the Balkans, and are known for their devotion to their owner. They are large animals, and generally very calm. Perhaps it's their size that makes them confident of not having to prove themselves by constant barking and agitated behavior, but they are fierce protectors of the flock, and do not hesitate to take on a wolf.

The nomads of former times have now mostly settled into fixed communities. They no longer crisscross the forbidding mountains of the Balkans in the seasonal migrations to fresh pasture, where these indomitable dogs defended man and beast alike. Today a handful of farmers still take their sheep through the mountains, following routes established many thousands of years ago, but modern farming methods have pretty much put an end to these traditions.

We twisted and turned our way ever downhill, the narrow road devoid of any traffic but for a tractor chugging along. We waved, the driver nodded as we carefully passed him. Down, down, steeply down we drove, the mountain almost always in sight keeping an eternal eye over the sea at its feet. The fields were parched. Brown and listless, patiently waiting for the rains which would restore them, with here and there a straggly plant trying to eke out an existence. Only the clumps of maquis looked healthy in their tangles of vibrant green, sharing the slopes with the silvery green of the olive trees. I hoped it was going to be a good harvest.

A sharp turn brought us to a tightly restricted part of the road, hemmed in on both sides by cars parked in front of houses. We had reached the fringes of the village. And a very pretty entrance it was. Oleander and bougainvillea seemed locked in mighty struggle to envelop the roadway, reaching over walls and fences to cross to the other side.

"The residents here must have to cut back constantly. Look how the growth has almost made a tunnel in this bit."

"Maybe they leave it deliberately because it provides shade for their cars?" Ron made his way slowly through the colorful plant and vehicle confusion. "This was never meant to handle vehicles. It must have been a donkey trail, a *kalderimi*."

Down and still down, the road narrowing even further as we began to approach the water.

❖ ❖ ❖

"Oh boy! Who goes where now?" Rounding the corner at the bottom of the incline was a large pickup truck which completely filled the road, barely making the turn between two sturdy walls on either side. But that was the least of it.

I gasped as a trailer came into view. "He's towing a boat! Ye gods! He's got a boat!" Indeed he had, a very large boat on a trailer, and suddenly the sleepy little lane, encased in attractive stone walls, trees and shrubbery, took on a rather intimidating air. "Where will we go? Which one of us must give way?"

The driver of the boat trailer and truck combo stopped and stared at us, making no gesture. No smile. No nod. Maybe he was as nonplussed as we. I couldn't imagine trying to negotiate that situation. It was like two adversaries engaged in hand to hand combat. Who would make the first move?

"Well, he's clearly not going to try reversing through that curve. I don't blame him. It's very difficult for him … no, I'm going to have to. It's alright, don't panic." Ron began to back the Elantra slowly up the very sharp incline. Judging by the noise the valiant little car was making, it was none too happy.

I clutched my knitting tightly, my eyes glued to the truck and boat combo which had begun to ascend. "Can't he wait, Ron? Why can't he wait? It's like he's forcing us back."

"He probably knows the road. Relax. There's an area coming up where I can pull over."

After a few more tense moments Ron was able to get off the road, much higher up, where he could pull off onto a small piece of flat ground and make it possible for the other driver to inch past us. He nodded tersely as he did so.

"He looked very nervous, Cathy, in all fairness. That was a bit stressful, I have to say."

The lane was clear again. Ron crept along while I held my breath, fearing a second confrontation with a boat and truck rig, but we reached the bottom with no further incident. The road opened into flat land a short distance from the water. There was ample parking space with a sandy beach on one side, and a generous parking area on the other. A couple of swimmers were taking a dip in the sparkling water which they had all to themselves.

"This is well off the beaten track, Ron. And the holiday period's over. I wonder if it's this quiet at the height of the season?"

"Maybe it's like Kalamos. It's not one of the main tourist destinations. Perhaps most of the visitors here are Greeks. Also it's not that easy to get to really, especially if you're coming from abroad."

"Well, Pelion is often described as being a well-kept secret. I love that it's so secluded."

The area along the waterfront is wider than the narrow road along the Kalamos beach, more open, with driveways leading inland from the water. A scattering of houses here and there, with well-kept gardens and a profusion of plants add to the sense of spaciousness, which is accentuated by the level ground.

"Oh look, Ron! We could have our own Shirley Valentine moment here."

Three tables were set out on the sandy beach, right at the edge of the water. One was occupied by a couple enjoying lunch, a second table was being cleared of the evidence of a large feast and much liquid refreshment, and the third was surely meant for us. Ron was able to park directly opposite, but he'd barely turned the engine off and I was out of the car to claim it lest anybody else showed up.

"I will come soon," a young woman told us in charmingly accented English as she walked across the street to deposit her laden tray inside a taverna.

"That tray's almost as big as she is, Ron. Heavy work."

'Ah, but she's young … here she comes."

"Welcome." She gave us each a menu. "What will you drink, please?"

She seemed a little surprised when I answered her in Greek. "Just two bottles of soda water, please. And for sure we'd like a *horiatiki*. And could we also have an additional piece of *feta*. We'll decide on a fish choice soon." She smiled and walked back across to the taverna. Built of stone, with a large veranda full of tables, with bougainvillea rambling in colorful abandon up the roof supports to praise the sun, it looked very inviting.

"What a location for a restaurant, Ron. So lovely. Anyway, I ordered a Greek salad, and also some extra feta. I think I'll have some *gavro*, and you? You want calamari or will you try something different?"

"No contest, calamari for me. Grilled."

Our sparkling water arrived, together with a bottle of still water and the typical basket of bread and the cutlery. The order given, we settled back to watch the sea dreaming at our feet.

"I could fall asleep here very easily, Ron. Just poke me with my knitting needle if I do."

"You won't be falling asleep now … you've first got to devour your tiny fried fish."

"Right. You know, I can't get over how calm the water is."

"Don't kid yourself. It can change in an instant. Many a sailor has drowned in these waters – even nowadays with all the modern equipment on boats. Lots of ancient vessels lie out there in these peaceful waters."

"Ron! Am I seeing things?" A duck came paddling by, a few feet from us, followed by her ducklings in an obedient line. "I've never seen anything like it!"

"She's clever, that mother duck," our server had arrived with the food at that moment, "she's hoping you'll throw her some bread. That's why she comes."

"But where does she come from? Is she from this taverna?" I'd noticed that the fish taverna adjoined a house where presumably the owners lived, rather like Vageli and Eleftheria.

"No, she appeared here a few weeks ago, but not with the babies. She must have made a nest somewhere, there's many places," she indicated the area behind the buildings fronting the road, "and then one day she was here with them."

My eyes were glued on her. "Ron, quickly, throw this piece of bread for her!" but mama duck and her brood had already sailed past.

"She can't be hungry, Cathy. There's probably lots to eat here. I reckon she's migratory – doesn't look like any domestic duck I know."

We piled our plates with salad. It was a very generous one, filled with plump black olives, topped by a thick slice of feta sprinkled with oregano.

I immediately sampled an olive. "Mmm, delicious. Very nice."

"These are my mother's," the young woman was pleased at my reaction. "People say she prepares the best table olives of anyone here in the village. She learnt how to do it from her mother."

"So, your family has been here a long time?" I had established her name, Lena, and continued asking her about the village. Ron, I noticed, was devouring his calamari. "Hands off my *gavro*, dear boy. I'm watching you. I'm learning a bit about Lefokastro. I'll explain it to you later."

The end of the road curved to the right, away from the beachfront, through the narrow gap between two houses; another point where pretty nimble driving would be required. Some lovely buildings were clustered along an embankment to the left, their grounds and balconies bright with colorful plants and cheerful awnings. I'm no geologist but the little bluff must have been carved out over millennia by the action of the sea. The same combination of wind and wave had created the waterfront where we were taking our ease. Several of the properties sported name signs which indicated that they were vacation rentals, and most attractive were they too. A taxi suddenly emerged from the right and drove up to one of the houses. The driver got out to offload the baggage whose owners were greeted enthusiastically by a woman coming down the steps to meet them.

"See over there, Ron, it's what you said about the area."

"What did I say about the area?"

"That it's difficult to get to, so that taxi over there means it's almost certainly not Greeks arriving there. It's people coming on holiday."

"Ah, Miss Marple, and how have you come to that conclusion?"

"Stop teasing me, Ron. They haven't come in their own car. Obviously. They've been brought here."

"Maybe their own car broke down? Or maybe they're returning home by taxi?"

"Just stop it!" and I helped myself to a very tasty piece of his calamari.

Lena appeared from across the road to bring us a plate of tiny ice cream cones.

"Po! Po! Lena. How did you know that this is quite the most perfect thing to round off a most perfect lunch?"

"I thought you'd like it. It's so hot today. But please don't leave because my father's coming soon to talk to you about our village. He knows a lot about it."

I translated for Ron. "Aren't we lucky that her father can spare the time to talk to us? I bet he'll be busy tonight."

"Yes, really good of him, but it helps that you speak Greek and are very interested in the history here."

Lena cleared away our plates, soon to return with her father whom she introduced to us as Andreas.

"*Kyrie* Andreas, my husband and I are delighted to meet you. Thank you very much for coming to talk to us. I have so many questions."

He pulled up a chair and we passed a pleasant half hour listening to his anecdotes. Lena, bless her, brought us more ice-cold water. I was secretly delighted that no further customers arrived to require his attention. He spoke a good

English. I congratulated him on his ability and he explained that he'd been a merchant seaman in his younger days. "I had the opportunity to learn. I was very lucky."

I'm not convinced that luck necessarily played any large part, but his knowledge of English would certainly be useful to him.

"So I saved my money and then came back here to my home village. I got married and with my wife, we opened this taverna. Our life is good. Now let me tell you about Lefokastro."

I asked him about the castle. He confirmed what I'd read in the guidebook, that confusion reigns about the name. Some sources claim that a white castle is the origin of the name, and others refer to an early settler by name of Lefas. If that's the case, that the structure was referred to as Lefas's castle, then in Greek Lefas, plus *kastro* is easily corrupted to Lefokastro.

"But what do you think? Do you think it was a person, or was the castle actually white? And when did this supposed Lefas settle here?"

Andreas shrugged. "There is a castle here, yes, a few bits of wall remain. They say it's from the medieval times, but me …"

I seized on his hesitancy. "Why would it have been medieval? That's comparatively recent time. Very recent. Look at those castles on Rhodes and other parts of Greece. They're medieval and most of them are in good condition. Why would the castle here have fallen into complete ruin?"

"I agree with you. There are many ancient sites here on Pelion. There are ruins of temples, for example. Here in Lefokastro there are bits and pieces from Classical times. And was it called a white castle because it was of marble? Maybe it was just stone, and painted white."

"Could it be, Andreas, that it was the stronghold of some powerful person? Not in ancient times, necessarily. Maybe somebody had a big house, well fortified. You know, like in the Peloponnese?"

"That could be so. Some people say he was a king."

"Maybe he was a king in ancient history. How will we know?"

Ron was anxious not to be a diversion. "Cathy, please speak in Greek to each other. I'm sure Andreas will be more comfortable. You can fill me in later."

Andreas smiled and nodded. We debated the subject a bit longer, finally agreeing that not enough research seems to have been done on a subject that greatly intrigues me. Perhaps the name really has nothing to do with its being white, and is simply a corruption of the name Lefas and *kastro*. Maybe this Lefas chap built himself a structure that could have withstood attack by pirates, and people referred to it as his castle. It makes sense that the settlement could eventually become known as Lefokastro. Whoever this Lefas was, and whether or not he built his castle on the ruins of some far earlier fortification, he had certainly availed himself of a site worthy of the gods who dwelt on the mountain above him. And quite possibly his building stones, whether he'd repurposed them or not, were still all around us, put to use yet again in some of the homes around us.

"So, what do you think of our village?"

"I love it, I think it's a perfectly gorgeous place, but that nasty corner at the bottom of the hill …" I trailed off.

"Oh yes, yes indeed," he chuckled, "but there's another even more difficult bit of road when you leave here and begin to drive into Afissos. Very difficult. A caravan got stuck up there once. It took days to free it. They had to bring a crane to get it out."

I relayed this cheery bit of information to Ron. "And Andreas says although it's quicker to go to Volos along this coastal road, it's better for us to stick to the top road. The main road."

A car pulled up behind ours, and a party of four headed to the empty tables. Excusing himself and wishing us well, Andreas returned to his taverna and Lena hurried to attend to the new arrivals.

"Here's the bill, I'll go in and pay it." Ron retrieved it from a small glass which Lena had put on the table earlier. When he returned he was carrying a plastic bag with some foil containers in it. "His wife gave me this. She says it's our leftovers."

We waved goodbye to Lena and returned to the car.

"Perhaps we should have stayed to watch the sunset, Ron, and do a Shirley Valentine. You know, drink a glass of wine where the grape is grown."

"Next time, when I'm more familiar with these roads."

"That was some meal. There's enough here for both of us to have later." I placed the bag of our leftovers on the rear seat as we climbed into the car. "We've still got cheese and fruit left if we need anything more to eat tonight."

WHICH WAY TO KALAMOS?

The Elantra made her way up the steep hill, with Ron making frequent gear changes and me busy knitting, but I could look around. It was as well that Ron kept his eyes on the road for a swirl of goats soon brought us to a standstill. Goats in great gaggles are a force to be reckoned with, particularly when trampling downhill. We waited. So did they. The gullies along the road provided rich pickings of plant life, as did the trees in which goats were clambering. A tree thick with hairy beasts sporting horns and very weird eyes, leaping about in seeming frenzy, is a disconcerting sight, but they finally moved on in a cacophony of bells and barking dogs.

"Up there," I indicated higher ground as we curved our way to the top of the hill, "I know you won't look, but all these large chunks of marble didn't just suddenly arrange themselves up here. This road's been cut into the hillside. There was something here … buildings … and the fields have been ploughed many times. Everything's smashed up, and much must have washed away over the centuries."

"Yes, there is a lot of broken marble around, now that you mention it. Large pieces."

"But Ron, given what we now know about Lefokastro, this was surely a site of significance. A temple, perhaps? It couldn't have been houses. Houses were of stone, mud, reeds in ancient times, not marble. People wanted materials that were easy to use, and also, I suppose, could be quite quickly erected. You have to cut marble, don't you? People lived in caves – there are caves all over the place around here – and there's no other spot with marble bits like these. The ground up here is flat, a perfect spot for a temple."

"Yes, you could be right, this would have been a good place for a temple. In honor of which god though? And when?"

"Well, if this was indeed a temple we're talking at least a couple of millennia ago, right? Maybe it was dedicated to Apollo? It's all so open, and spread so far and wide high over the sea …the sun would have been in the sky for many hours a day. And it sets right across there. A perfect place to praise him, Ron, don't you think?"

"Or possibly Artemis? There would have been excellent hunting here. Maybe this was a place to worship her. To keep her sweet so the hunting would be good?"

"I wonder if more about this spot will ever be known? You think? I'm convinced there's something here."

"There are a great many places that need excavation, Cathy, and Greece doesn't have much money to do it. What archaeologists have managed to discover and document so far is quite incredible, and remember they have to work through so much myth, confirmed history, local legends and such to establish facts."

We reached the *iconostasis.* The sheep had moved further down the hill. I didn't see the shepherd so he'd presumably left his tree and gone with them.

"I think I'll try this route to Kalamos. Shall we give it a go?"

"Fine," I continued counting stitches, and we turned off the tarred road onto the stony earthen track. The entrance to it was much narrowed by the dense maquis, but once we'd passed the shrine and gone a couple of hundred yards, it widened out, although only into a single lane. Open fields interspersed with olive groves spread out on either side as the trail wound ahead towards the Gulf, but soon we were hemmed in again by very dense maquis doing its best to strangle the roadway and recover the ground it had lost to the track. We bumped and thumped our tortuous way along through potholes and rocks, enveloped in clouds of dust.

"That's the outskirts of Argalasti," Ron pointed to the left where buildings were clustered beyond the open fields. No explanation was necessary with respect to the scene on the right where the mountain rises confidently to her full height, her villages scattered about her and her upper slopes dressed in the hardwoods for which Mt. Pelion has been known for millennia.

Ron pulled up as far to the side of the track as he could, though it hardly appeared that much traffic would be hurtling through. "This is a good spot if you want to get out and take some photos, and if I'm not mistaken we're more or less parallel to where you commented about the marble. Look, there's bits of marble in these fields too, and this ground's quite flat. Good land for corn or wheat most likely. A temple would have taken up valuable land. That's if you're right about that. This has been farmed, ploughed repeatedly through many years. The marble's been broken up again and again. The people needed the ground for crops."

I got out with my camera and walked a few feet into the field. Each step I took stirred up dust from the parched ground.

"Take your time, and then I'm going to turn round and go back the way we came. Sorry, Cathy, but this road is so bad that I really can't risk damaging the car. It needs a four-wheel drive. And this is the dry season. I can't imagine what it's like in the winter downpours."

"Why are you sorry? It's no problem for me. And you're right about the car. Those car hire guys would have a fit."

"Over there's a place I can turn round – it looks to be leading to that tin shed down there."

I settled myself back in the car. Ron drove on a few yards, made a multi-point turn in the footpath, and we drove back to the shrine and the reassurance of a tarred road, patched in places though it was.

Argalasti was beginning to come to life as we drove through the main street. The afternoon rest was over. Shops were slowly opening up. Tavernas were preparing for the busy evening hours with tables being wiped down and chairs rearranged. There wasn't a breath of air. Not a leaf stirred.

"Can you stop here a moment please, Ron. I'm going to see if I can get some ice cream in the grocery shop."

"It's so hot that a tub will melt very quickly in the car. Get individual ones we can eat as we drive back."

I chose two ice cream cones and paid with the largest denomination drachma note in my purse, nervous of trying to count out the required amount. In spite of the air conditioning in the car we had to eat quickly or be dripping with ice cream. I shoved my knitting safely into its bag.

"I think this must be the hottest day we've had so far," I wiped my chin with a tissue. "This chocolate affair's really very good."

ZEUS THROWS A TANTRUM

We turned down the Kalamos road. Something caught my eye. Far out to sea, at the rim of the western horizon, tiny white dots divided water from sky. The effect was of an enormous coverlet of tie-dyed blue fabric, edged with a white bobbled fringe.

"See that, Ron. That's caused by the wind, right?"

"Coming straight from the west, yes. It's way out. All's still calm here. Interesting. I can't tell if it's coming this way."

The further down the road we moved, the faster the wind-rippled water advanced. By the time we were driving along the Kalamos beachfront, the white bobbles had become long streaks of seething white water. Behind them was a newcomer in the form of a billowing band of purple black cloud, angrily shoving at the water as the furiously foaming mass reached the shore. The wind gained strength extremely rapidly and when we pulled up near Bakaloni's, it was thrashing the olive trees, flaying the ground and shrieking in triumph as it hurled debris through the air. The sea was a gigantic foam bath, spindrift spitting salt into our faces. Bakaloni opened the door as we passed – hanging on to it – and yelled at us to get quickly to Magda's.

"It was too hot! This is a bad storm! Hurry! Hurry! Get inside!"

We needed no urging and raced across the sand to Magda's house where waves had already flooded the courtyard. We dashed indoors and slammed the door shut. Anxious though I'd been when we'd left the car, I'd still retained enough of my wits to remember both the knitting and the food, which I placed on the kitchen table.

"I guess you'll not say no to tea." Ron was already putting the kettle on. "I don't know if we'll lose electricity, but at least this is gas."

"Thanks."

"I'd better check the shutters ... stay here."

Although it wasn't yet 6:00 o'clock, the sky had darkened enough that we needed to switch on the dim lights. The lightning flashes lit up the kitchen in eerie neon colors; I felt I was in some kind of stage setting for a drama of murder and mayhem.

The sea competed with the thunder, each roaring in a relentless barrage of noise while rain battered in fury on the roof.

"Do you think the roof's going to hold, Ron? What if it gets blown off? What if it leaks."

"I think it will be alright. There's some protection from the trees. Not much really ... it's all coming at us head on. We'll be OK, don't worry. The shutters rattle a bit but they're holding."

Ron had placed some of the rag rugs against the door where they kept the water from coming in. I wondered if the whole house would be flooded, and what kind of damp mess would ensue.

"The gods are still up on the mountain. It's their summer home … Zeus must be furious with Hera, livid." I took a sip of my tea. "He's obviously chased one nymph too many through the trees and he's had enough of Hera's shouting at him. Not that I blame her. What an awful row they're having."

Ron laughed. "So now he's letting his displeasure be known."

"And how. He's flinging his thunderbolts all around, and has called up his cronies."

"His cronies?"

"Yes. Poseidon's doing his bidding and churning up the sea, but first Zeus commanded Aeolus to unleash his winds. So here we sit now because Zeus couldn't keep it in his pants."

"You do tell a good story, Cathy. So how long for him to calm down?"

"Well, I can't be sure. When I was a little kid in South Africa my Mother would tell me slightly edited versions of some of the myths when she thought it appropriate. You know what terrible thunderstorms we get there, so my Mother would say that Zeus was a bit angry with his wife, Hera, because he didn't like her food or something, and then he'd behave very badly and cause all kinds of trouble, and poor Hera was very long-suffering and put up with it. I loved her stories, but once I could read she had a bit of explaining to do."

"I bet she did, Cathy, I bet she did!"

The lights began to flicker. "Hmm, I don't want to be stumbling around in the dark. Where's your torch, your flashlight? I think I saw some candles here in the kitchen. Yes, there, Ron, up on that shelf. We'd better keep them handy."

"There's a couple of oil lamps here too, so no problem even if the lights do go out. Nothing to worry about. More tea?"

"Please." I applied myself to my knitting. "Are you hungry? That's a lot of food we were given to bring home. Have it."

Ron opened the foil containers. "Oh, look, she's given us a whole tub of those delicious olives. How very nice of her. Bread and olives … that's all I want. What can I get you?"

'Nothing thanks. I suppose it's quite cozy here in the kitchen, but where would one sit in the winter? The courtyard's hardly for winter use."

"They probably didn't stay here all through the winter. Didn't Magda tell you they would go back to Argalasti after the harvest?"

"Yes, she did. I wonder what the Argalasti house is like? Perhaps it's more modern."

"Well, maybe we'll see it one day."

The electricity held its own. By the time we went to bed the thunder and lightning had begun to lessen, as had the wind. The storm was moving away, but the rain had no intention of doing so and continued into daybreak. Only then did it too disappear.

AFTER THE STORM

"That was quite a night, that was. I don't need Zeus to pitch another hissy fit like that again, Ron."

"Well, everyone has been talking of the unusual heat, so I guess it was inevitable. I'm surprised the roof didn't leak, I must say, and I don't think we lost any tiles. Look, let's get breakfast done, and then we'll head up to the email tree. You get a good view from there, so maybe we can see if there was any damage."

There were a few small branches scattered about. Leaves and flowers littered Magda's courtyard which was full of large puddles. Seawater? Rainwater? A mixture of both, no doubt. Seaweed was piled up on the sand, threaded through with shells and the infuriating mess of plastic which pollutes the world, even to the remotest of corners. Pieces of green sea glass, wave-bashed bits of beer bottles, glittered in the sun. Tin cans and bottles were heaped against the chicken wire fence which distinguished Magda's little front yard from the narrow public beach. The ground was very wet, making it difficult to keep our footing as we trudged up the bank, but otherwise we saw nothing significant. The sea, an agitated mass of white water, was still fuming at having been so stirred up by the frenzy of Zeus and his cohorts, the little boats at anchor on her bobbing about in bewilderment.

"I thought the water would be calmer, but it isn't. Seems odd because there's not that much wind now."

"The water takes quite a bit longer to settle down, Cathy. The wave action will continue for a while still."

"Well, considering what Poseidon and his cronies have managed to do, let's hope Zeus doesn't get into another argument while we're still here. Last night was more than enough."

We reached the email tree. "Just look at that, Ron! It must be the river." A wide swath of muddy water stretched from Kalamos into the middle of the Pagasitic. The sea, white water frothing through its brilliant blues and greens, was bisected by the swift flow of mud. "That's all runoff. That water's carrying an enormous amount of soil. It's being lost forever. Awful!"

"Yes, but some of it gets deposited at sea-level. Over the centuries it builds up, it alters the landscape. Can be good … can be bad. In some circumstances flooding can be beneficial. Think of the Nile."

But I didn't want to think of the Nile. I could focus only of what the storm might have done to the area, and already some damage was apparent from the large branches strewn about the hillside. "Those are olives - the trees have been hammered."

"It's wide open up here. Completely exposed. The wind must have been very strong to do this, but the olive has endured plenty through the millennia of its cultivation. The trees will survive. Nature has lent a hand with the pruning."

"I suppose."

"Cheer up Cathy, by some miracle communications haven't been disrupted … the emails are downloading, no trouble."

Back at Magda's we debated what to with the day. "Ron, I know we'd planned to hike but maybe that's not such a good idea with the ground so wet. What do you think?"

" Well, the sun will have it all dried out by tomorrow. We can go then. What do you want to do today?"

"What about we go into Volos? We've seen nothing of it at all."

"Good point. Makes sense. It will be nice to get an idea of where Jason and his Argonauts departed from."

"I know it sounds silly, Ron, but Jason and his crew are beginning to seem real to me. The guide book shows the harbor. The waterfront looks interesting too. Maybe have lunch there? Or perhaps we should rather eat at Galini's tonight? It would be nice to speak to Eleftheria and Vageli."

"Let's just see how we feel as the day progresses. I need to send some emails, but no need to do that yet … everybody's asleep there now. What about you? Do you need to send any of your book stuff today?"

"No, but I must knit as much as I can, and as fast as I can. No worries."

We readied ourselves and set off for the car. Walking towards Bakaloni's along the beach that morning was a very different experience to that of the previous evening when we were racing to get back to the house. There was no wind. There was no lightning. No deafening claps of thunder. The path along the sandy beach was not there. Indeed, the sandy beach was not there. In its place was an ankle-wrenching mass of rocks and stones, broken bottles and intact bottles, piles and piles of fishing nets, great heaps of leaves, branches and logs and pieces of wood, plastic in the form of bags, bottles and sundry objects. All of it wet. All of it ugly.

The Bakalonis were in front of their shop, sweeping sand and pebbles off the concrete and back down onto the beach, shoveling trash into heaps to dump into buckets and cardboard boxes. Both were well advanced in years. Both were very tired.

"Is there anything we can do?" My question sounded feeble to my ears, but it begged to be asked.

"No, thank you. Someone's coming soon to help us. We'll manage. Were you alright? Has Magda's house been damaged?"

We assured them that all was well, that we were sorry they had such a mess to deal with.

"*Kalimera*!" a voice sang out. "*Po! Po! Po!*"

Hurrying towards us was Costa, the friendly chap of the walnuts.

"*Olla kala. Olla kala.*"

This literally means "all is well" but it was uttered in the sense of reassurance: "I am here. Do not worry." The good soul took the broom from *kyria* Katina's hands and swept vigorously away.

"Can we bring you anything?"

"*Ochi, ochi,* thank you, but be careful. Have a good day."

The car was plastered with plant debris, but was otherwise undamaged. I climbed in while Ron cleared the windshield. "I see why people don't live right on the water during the winter. Must be why some of these houses are already shuttered up … the summer season's over."

Ron started the car. "It seems storms like this aren't typical here in summer, but it's moving into winter now. Like in Texas, the worst time of the year for storms."

We drove along the narrow lane that masquerades as a road. Branches and twigs littered the way as we approached the bridge. The previous day the river's course had been a dry bed, having only a little tidal seawater in it as it reached the shore. Not so this day.

The river raced, thick with mud, out into the Pagasitic, just as we had seen it from the email tree. We crossed the river, I feeling more than a little nervous because of the fast-flowing water below. We continued along the waterfront which was as full of debris as it was on our side of the river, with small rocks and garbage hurled from the sea right up onto the roadway.

"I need to be careful of broken glass. Cathy, keep a lookout for it, please."

"Some folk have a lot of cleaning up to do, for sure. These front yards are full of stones and stuff. I guess it's the price they pay for being only feet from the water. I wonder how often this happens?" I glanced at the knitting in my lap – that at least I can control.

We turned the corner at the end of the beaten-up beach and headed towards Argalasti. Signs of storm damage began to lessen the higher up we drove, but it certainly had rained very hard as shown by the water gushing downhill to the sea. Gutters were overflowing in Argalasti. Great pools of water lined the roadside.

We passed the turnoff to Lefokastro. "Hard to believe that we were here just a few hours ago … and now, it's much cooler, Ron, for one thing."

"I wonder what that dirt track to Kalamos looks like after all the rain. I bet it's a mess."

"I wasn't paying a great deal of attention when we first arrived, but isn't this road tarred all the way to Volos?"

"Yes, we shouldn't have any problems."

MEANDERING TO VOLOS

Ron swerved to avoid a branch in our path, driving through an enormous puddle as he did so. Water ran down onto the road from embankments along the way, while here and there a miniature rainbow glistened briefly as the sun shone on the cascades. The tempestuous Pagasitic was still tossing its vivid sapphire and emerald colors about, but from the height we were at the white water appeared to be lessening.

The drive to Volos lasted about an hour during which time Ron hardly took his eyes off the road. Not only was it as twisty as a snake in many parts, but most of the drivers seemed to be imagining themselves the reincarnation of Fangio, and those few who didn't were imitating snails. The ones that made me the most nervous were elderly drivers gripping the steering wheel as they crept along, peering ahead. Throw in the odd donkey cart, tractors, and some strange three-wheeled affairs and you really did need to keep your driving wits about you. As for seethings of sheep and great congregations of goats, well, we'd started to realize that these are daily hazards in the rural scheme of things and began to handle them in our stride.

The road we were traveling on is the Peninsula backbone, running from the outskirts of Volos down to *Aghia Kyriaki*. That is to say, it's the main artery. Looking at maps later, Ron reckoned one can probably get from one end to the other in a vehicle by dint of travel entirely along side roads, by zigging and zagging from the east coast to the west coast of the peninsula, crossing the unforgiving terrain in off-road vehicles to achieve that goal. "It wouldn't be easy … not getting onto the main road at all … but it can probably be done. I don't know if there's a vehicle that could actually do it. Horse, donkey, trail bike, yes that could, but if you used a combination of those and a motorized vehicle it defies the concept of a conventional car making the journey."

"But it would take forever to get there like that, Ron … maybe even more than a day."

"Well, you could undertake it as a hike. Quite a challenge … where you never set foot on the main road. You would have the most fantastic trek. Just think of it. The views would be mind-blowing. The things you could discover."

"Hmm, you could certainly attempt it, maybe one day, but don't even think of including me in such a venture. Cathy of the Kalderimi I am not."

We weren't thinking of that as we drove along however. While Ron, in his own words was "trying to keep us alive", I had the luxury of uninterrupted viewing of the landscape, the surroundings and Mt. Pelion, and only Ron's exclamations, together with some rather frequent swerving, brought my thoughts back to the road.

"When we were driving to Argalasti the day we arrived, well, you were driving, I didn't pay much attention to this road. I was so busy gazing at the sea that it didn't dawn on me that the road is so full of curves."

"Yes, and dangerous they are too. Blind curves, and lots of places that you can fall right off the road."

I shivered. "And people seem inclined to stop just anywhere. Look at him, for example." With his car parked barely to the side of the road a man was relieving himself behind it. This is not an uncommon sight in parts of Europe and while the action itself is of little or no concern to the average motorist, the choice of impromptu rest stop is often not a well-considered one.

Mt. Pelion and its foothills are visible for a good part of the journey into Volos from the Peninsula. Beautiful. Stunningly beautiful. You have to be without soul or greatly preoccupied not to be struck by it. For a large part of the ride the Pagasitic lies to your left, sometimes far below as you descend from the height of the Peninsula, and then not far from the road as you reach the coastline. The gales of the previous night had eased into a strong breeze which sailing vessels were taking advantage of. Most of these had white sails, particularly the bigger yachts, their billowing sheets of canvas creating interesting patterns among the white caps of the waves, like thinly spread whipped cream on a pie. Some of the smaller boats sported red sails, little strawberries on a gigantic cake.

The strong winds and heavy downpours of the previous day had cleared the air of dust and smoke. The mountain sparkled in the tight embrace of the cloudless sky that surrounded it and the deep, deepest blues of the sea at its feet. The villages nestled on its slopes stood out sharply, much more conspicuous than they had appeared through the haze of the previous days, their windows and roofs visible against the whitewashed walls. This much at least had the storm achieved.

◆ ◆ ◆

The guide book told us that Mt. Pelion has twenty four villages, dating through antiquity from the Paleolithic to the modern age. Where there was water in the form of springs there would be people gathering for the easy access to it, not to mention for food. Game was abundant in ancient times; the animals were also in search of fresh water. I imagine that there might have been other villages which have since disappeared as the water source dried away, but Mt. Pelion is very well-watered so others would have sprung up. The mountain is still heavily forested, particularly on the highest slopes, in spite of the fact that it was a major source of timber for the building of boats since Man first figured out he could improve upon a log to move through the water.

Mt. Pelion arises from the plains of Thessaly, a region known since antiquity for its horses, and takes its name from the mythical king Peleus. It extends into a peninsula which shelters the Pagasitic Gulf from the open waters of the Aegean Sea to the east, while the mainland protects it from the west. No doubt geologists can explain in great detail how the Gulf was formed through the aeons, but it seems to me that perhaps what is now the Gulf was an ancient lake or river at one time. People might well have lived along its banks, possibly peoples of whom we have no knowledge. Their civilizations might have been destroyed by the forces of Nature. Earthquakes must surely have played a role in this earthquake-prone region, as well might have catastrophic flood. Once breached, either by the river flowing into the Mediterranean or the other way around, humans could find their way to it.

◆ ◆ ◆

Those first arriving in the region of Pelion enjoyed a comfortable existence. The weather is not harsh. Game abounded. Fresh water was abundant. The fruits of the sea were plentiful. Man's ingenuity knows no bounds, and these most ancient of the area's ancestors would have made themselves as comfortable as they needed to be. Life was surely good and, given the wealth of archeological evidence attesting to daily existence through many millennia, it continued to be.

To tell of the area's beauty requires songs of praise worthy of the venerable bards of old. Simply put, and at the risk of becoming repetitive, it's awesome. It's here on this mountain that some authorities believe the Greek myths originated; others hold to the opinion that the source was Crete. The first spinners of these stories were trying to explain their world. They were deep thinkers, the earliest of philosophers. How had their world come to be and how did it function? Why was there day, and why was there night? What was the moon? What was the sun? Why was there a time of warmth when food was plentiful, and why a time of difficult cold?

They explained these concepts in terms all could understand by attributing human behaviors to invisible beings. How else could they have done so for how little of the world, indeed the universe, was known to them? The span of time involved boggles the mind. How long did it take for the creation stories to make their way from Crete – if that was the case – to Pelion? They must have been brought by brave sea-faring people. And wherever the birthplace of these enthralling narratives might be, for how long were the myths being created, told and retold, added to and embroidered? Were many lost forever, or were some absorbed into other tales?

But there is no mystery as to why these wonderful anthologies have survived through the millennia. The myths were the soap operas of the day, capturing the imagination. The stories are fascinating – full of intrigue, of daring heroes and wily traitors. They tell of thrilling adventures, of monumental victories and of terrible destruction, of great passions and of dastardly betrayals. The themes would have been familiar, for those who heard the stories of triumph and achievement, of loss, defeat and death, could identify in some way through their own experience.

The myths dominated every aspect of life, providing a degree of explanation for the human condition. People would have gathered, eager to hear the latest episode about the gods and their messy lives, their love affairs, their misdeeds, as well as their many acts of kindness. They paid tribute to their gods; they made sacrifice. The exploits of the gods featured prominently in their art, executed with skill and imagination, from vase painting to great works of marble.

A visitor to a community might bring a fresh tale, and maybe take one away to others when resuming his journey. The Greeks were and still are renowned for their hospitality, their care of the foreigner. Zeus himself was held up as the protector of strangers to whom all kindness should be extended. Who knew if the stranger might not be a god in disguise? Ancient Greek gods are unlikely to show up in Greek company these days, but the concept of a warm welcome remains a hallmark of Greek life.

The mythological centaurs, depicted with the head and torso of a man and the body of a horse, cavorted about on the slopes of the mountain. Various Greek myths attempt to explain their origin. Given that horses abounded on the lush plain of Thessaly and so were known to prehistoric man, it's not difficult to conclude how the myth of the centaurs might have begun. Some confused soul could have seen a man on horseback, clinging to the horse's neck. Perhaps the viewer's eyesight was poor, or his perception affected by a little too much of an intoxicating substance. He would hasten to tell his story. The news would spread. The idea of such a creature as a centaur might thus have come into being, became a part of the mythology, and was accepted without question by people who had no other frame of reference.

Centaurs were regarded as a troublesome, uncouth bunch, with the exception of the centaur Chiron, who was learned and honorable. Chiron is sometimes represented as having the forelegs of a human rather than those of a horse, a reference to the fact that he was born of a more refined branch of the family. He raised Asclepius, who was later to become the god of medicine, teaching him all that he knew of medicine and surgery. Chiron's reputation as a scholar was so great that many of those who feature in the Greek fables came to his cave to be tutored by him. Jason, who sought the Golden Fleece, was one such notable character.

Among Chiron's attributes was his knowledge of medicinal herbs which grow abundantly in Pelion. The slopes of the mountain are a botanist's dream, luxuriant with an enormous variety of plants, of which several are exceedingly rare. Large areas of lush vegetation conceal caves yet to be discovered and which may still be guarding Neolithic paintings and artifacts. Water, cold and pure, springs from rocks into pools where the keen hiker may be refreshed. You can imagine yourself to be alone on the mountain as you trek through the wildflowers, shaded by canopies of trees where unseen birds chirp and sing. A sudden movement may catch your eye, and for a second you fancy a centaur slipped behind a boulder, only to have your daydream rudely shattered when you spy the ugly piece of litter agitating in the breeze.

◆ ◆ ◆

We drove though little villages on our way to Volos, passing signs directing visitors to beaches and various types of accommodation, as well as to tavernas and coffee shops. Occasionally a sign would be written in English, but for the most part they were in Greek – package holiday tour operators hadn't yet arrived in Pelion in any numbers. There were several bakeries fronting the road, the tantalizing aromas a great temptation to stop and sample and when we at times did, to buy far too much of the delicious breads and goodies. Pharmacies, immediately noticeable by their flashing green cross signs, seemed to be doing brisk business, together with some establishments announcing themselves to be mini-markets. These looked to be along the lines of a general store and included everything from garden tools and furniture out in the front, and groceries indoors. Together with the butcher shops and numerous roadside fruit and vegetable stalls, they could provide pretty much what the locals needed.

As we approached Volos, the traffic began to thicken, fed by folk in an assortment of vehicles coming from the beachfront areas and down from villages on the mountain slopes. Most of the cars were old, and most of them were quite beaten up, not to mention rusted. I noted that many were Ladas.

"They're very basic, Cathy, and cheap. They do the job. It's not as if there are *autobahns* here to drive on ... how fast can you go?"

"That doesn't seem to be a problem for those guys," I replied as two lads – no helmets – roared past on motorbikes, weaving in most dangerous fashion between vehicles. Puddles of water and overflowing gutters indicated that the storm of the previous night hadn't spared the area, but the sun was bright and people were bustling about their business.

"I've noticed a couple of Jimny's. Those would be very good in these areas."

"What's a Jimny?"

"It's that over there, Cathy. See? A small 4WD - Suzuki makes them. Very practical. A good utility vehicle."

"Well, these moped things seem popular ... a bit dangerous though, I would think."

"Especially as nobody's wearing a crash helmet," Ron slowed down to avoid a car parked in the street directly in front of a bakery. To complicate matters the passenger door was open, blocking the sidewalk. As we slowly passed by, I caught a glimpse of a child climbing into the offending car with a loaf of bread sticking out of a paper bag under his arm and an ice cream cone in his hand.

The road widened as we moved away from the cluster of shops. We were driving close to the sea through an area of waterfront coffee shops and restaurants. Very pretty. Very enticing.

"Ye gods! What's that?" A monstrously ugly complex of industrial buildings, hideous towers of concrete and rusted metal, belching black smoke from evil-looking chimneys rose up in front of us, all set against the towering walls of a quarry.

'Ah, yes. The cement factory. An eyesore if ever there was one. You didn't see it when we came through here from Athens … I think you'd dozed off."

"I can't bear to look at it. And there, those funny boats … what are they?" Docked in front of the factory were cargo vessels of some type.

"They're designed to carry concrete. Those cranes are loading it."

We fell silent. Modern life and modern needs. Such ugliness, slap bang in the middle of an exquisite area, glaring out over water saturated with the history of millennia.

The factory disappeared from view as we moved on. Further up the road, in sharp contrast to the industrial grime, swimmers were taking a dip in the sparkling waters. A small group appeared to be in training for something. A man in a rowing boat, a coach probably, gave instructions to the youngsters plying the oars in small craft around him. Seated on the grassy verge nearby, a family of gypsies offered vegetables and plants for sale from supplies in the back of a small truck. Fitness enthusiasts jogged along, cyclists flying past them, while others limbered up in readiness for whatever form of exercise they planned. I knitted on steadily.

WANDERING AND WONDERING IN VOLOS

We drove into the port city of Volos, turning into Demetriados street where we immediately came upon an empty lot doing service as a car park.

"We're in luck! I don't have to hunt for parking."

Ron was quite right. Finding a parking space in the street looked very unlikely, particularly as we had no real idea of where we were going. The attendant indicated where Ron should park. He paid the man, we gathered up our things and set off. "Right, there's the sea ... looks busy. Shall we head there first?"

We crossed at the traffic light and made our way through to the waterfront. The University of Thessaly buildings occupy a prime spot on the promenade – a very attractive area with lots of space to stroll, lined with eateries and coffee shops of all kinds. Navigating through the inevitable hawkers of trinkets and pirated CDs, we made our way towards the ferry port from where one can access the islands of the Sporades.

"Imagine how it must be at the height of the season." I shook my head as yet another hopeful thrust a contraption filled with tickets at me. "*Ochi, ochi.*" At first I thought they were ferry tickets but I soon learned they're for the national lottery.

"*Kalimera*!" Many a pleasant soul invited us to be seated at a cafe or the like but we weren't in need of refreshment and politely reciprocated the greetings as we continued walking. The ringing of church bells led us to turn up a side street and soon we were in the main business and shopping area. The church of St Nicholas, a fine example of Byzantine church architecture, dominates this part of the city. There's a small plaza in front of it where mothers pushed prams and tended to excited kiddies, where people sat on benches, some eating a snack from the busy take-away shops nearby, some deep in conversation or quietly reading, while the ever-present pigeons trod about underfoot in hopes of a morsel. The devout invariably crossed themselves as they passed the church, occasionally one popped in to light a candle, or to remain a while in solitary reflection.

We sat on the low wall surrounding the plaza, I knitting as we watched. The activity, the noise, wasn't in any way a distraction, but rather an affirmation that people go about their affairs whatever the circumstances.

Stepping back into the pedestrianized street, we ambled along amongst a sizeable crowd, dodging and being dodged by cyclists. The shops were most interesting. There was a delightfully old-fashioned grocery store where dried goods were scooped from large sacks into paper bags. When the customer was satisfied with the quantity, it was carefully weighed, the total price calculated and written in pencil on the bag. You paid for your purchases at the exit.

Nearby a small shop offered textiles ranging from socks and stockings, underwear and petticoats, shirts and blouses, children's clothes and baby outfits, to various household essentials like towels and dishcloths. But what caught my eye was the large range of aprons hanging outside, where they swung to and fro in the breeze. Bright and cheerful, classic bib-fronted aprons in a plethora of colorful designs, there was something very heartwarming about them. Several years later, the humble apron would come into vogue again to the delight of sewing enthusiasts and book publishers alike.

❖ ❖ ❖

There were no department stores in Volos at that time, nor for that matter any large stores. Shoe shops abounded, as they still do, with a huge range of the most gorgeous shoes. The leather industry has always been well supported in Greece. We saw several little shops dealing in ready-made leather clothing, but also offering custom work; quality was of a very high standard. What did please me greatly were the tiny little cobbler shops, all very busy. I popped into one where I was able to find just the right shade of red shoe polish for a favorite pair of ankle boots. It seems such a trivial purchase but I was delighted with it, and in fact still use it all these years later. The young man who sold it to me, son of the owner, was most solicitous, making sure I was describing the right shade of red. Considering that I was not going to be making any large purchase from a repair shop, and that he would likely not see me, a tourist again, his customer service was impeccable.

We chatted a bit about the demise of traditional cobblers in so much of the Western world.

"If you have a good pair of shoes," he remarked, "they will last a long time. It's important to take care of them, and repair them when there's a problem. If you look after your shoes, you won't need to waste your money on new ones for no reason."

Well, yes, I saw his point, but I doubt he'd factored in the lure of the fashion industry.

"Shall we have something to drink, Ron?" I'd noticed tall glasses of iced coffee being enjoyed at pavement cafes as we meandered along. "It's getting hot and those look good."

" Where shall we go? You want to walk back to the waterfront, or somewhere here?"

"No, back to the water, please. It's so lovely there."

❖ ❖ ❖

The side streets of Volos are an Aladdin's cave of treasures and surprises for me. The shops are small, often crammed with unusual items. There are the tiniest of boutiques showcasing one-of-a-kind clothing, others offering handmade shoes and bags. The handcrafted jewelry is always worth a look, as are the art galleries. Vintage furniture is often part of the shop fittings, displaying merchandise to best advantage, though usually it's those antique tables and cabinets that draw my eye. We strolled along, admiring the profusion of goods. Goodies too. The most tempting of sweetmeats, imaginatively displayed that surely only the most self-controlled can resist.

"Just look at these chocolates! Look at their shapes! I'm going to get some for Eleftheria. Let's go eat there tonight." I selected some. The assistant put them into a box which she tied up most elegantly with ribbon.

"Aren't you going to get any for yourself?"

"No, I'm already putting on weight."

Ron shrugged and paid out the *drachma* and on we walked. Tucked into alcoves and corners here and there outside of coffee shops and restaurants, small seating arrangements are set up where you can enjoy your drink or meal should you choose not to sit inside. Often just a mini table and two chairs. A boon in those days prior to the indoor smoking ban, but we passed them by.

And then we came upon a bookshop and were undone. Irresistible. No way could we ignore it. A very good selection of books was carefully arranged on shelves. Bestsellers in Greek were prominently displayed and included translations of recent English bestselling authors, mostly thrillers and crime. A comprehensive selection of popular novelists, foreign dictionaries, poetry, coffee table books, as well as a large range of children's books, catered for most types of the reading public. I could have stayed there all day, especially among the offerings for kids. Several of these were published in Greece, but many of the great English and French children's classics were available in translated Greek editions. Very encouraging. Greeks prize education.

"Found anything?" Ron was holding a thick book and a map.

"Yes, I like this – see, it's all about the history of Magnesia and it's in English. Been translated from the Greek. The photos are stunning."

Ron looked at it. "*Magnesia: The Story of a Civilization.* That looks very interesting. The Neolithic settlements … there's a lot to learn here. Good find, Cathy."

We left with our bag of books which Ron carried, together with the chocolates, while I knitted beside him as we walked the short distance to the water. Soon we were settled at a table on the promenade, iced coffees ordered, watching the world go by. Busy and noisy it was, but not at all unpleasant, and the coffee was very refreshing. The seagulls, those most troublesome of seafront birds, swept about screeching and squawking, dive-bombing the fishing boats, oblivious to the more sedate pigeons strutting among the tables in their superior manner.

"Do you want another coffee?"

I shook my head.

"Let's get going then. I'd like to take a look at the boats in harbor."

A very large fishing *caïque* was offloading its catch just beyond the administrative buildings and ferry terminals of the harbor complex, the frenetic gulls adding to the commotion. We watched for a bit, then turned away to explore the fish market.

DOING A JASON

"Yikes! Ron! Ron, my shoe …" The sole of my shoe had decided to part company with the rest of it, and was flapping about rather like the fish in the nets. "Look, it's broken into two pieces! How could this have happened?"

"Let me look." Ron placed our bags down on a convenient bench. An old fellow seated on one end of it stared at us.

"I don't know what's gone wrong here, Cathy. Must have been a production flaw … these are quite new, aren't they?"

"You bet and not cheap either! I can't walk like this – my foot's touching the ground. The whole thing's coming apart. What can I do?"

"Well, first off, sit down here." Ron guided me to the bench, I hopping along with the remains of the sandal hanging from my foot. The old man continued to stare as Ron retrieved the broken pieces and put them in his backpack. "Can you ask the chap to move a bit so I can sit down, please Cathy?"

But he'd already begun to shuffle away, leaning on his stick. "We've chased him off, Ron. Poor old thing."

"There's plenty more benches. He must have thought it best to leave us crazy foreigners to it."

We examined the shoe.

"I don't know Cathy, I can only think of two solutions. I'll go back to that cobbler's shop with this and see what he can do while you wait here.

You've got your knitting – or we can try to find a shoe store and get something else."

"I don't really see what he can do, Ron. He can't glue or nail this back on because it's badly split, and anyway part of the upper has been torn away with it."

Ron nodded. "I don't think there's any way this can be repaired."

I looked around. "I can't see anything here. No shops, only eateries and such. We'll need to go up to the main shopping area and I don't know how I'll be able to walk. I'm not putting my bare foot on the ground. Ugh!"

"Then I'll go fetch the car and we'll go back to Magda's."

"No wait, I'm thinking. See that over there," I pointed to a kiosk a few yards away from us, "it sells all kinds of things and I see sunhats hanging up."

"Sunhats? What do you want a sunhat for? Haven't you got one?"

"We can wrap it around my foot – I can use some of my knitting yarn to tie it on – and you can help me totter along to find a shop. Better still, the pharmacies all seem to sell Dr Scholl-type sandals. A pair of those will do me fine. Or perhaps a pair of flip flops. There may even be some at the kiosk."

Ron seemed doubtful. "You think? Why don't I leave you here and see what I can find?"

"And even if you do, will you find my size? It's getting late in the season and maybe they'll be sold out. And anyway, what time is it? Doesn't everything close up soon?"

"You're right. That woman's shutting up her kiosk already. Alright, I'll go get a hat quickly. Won't be long."

I could see him and the kiosk lady examining hats and soon he was back with a baseball cap. "You can put your foot into this, and see these eyelets along the visor – I can tie it on your foot somehow. And also there's these adjustable side straps … let me have some of your yarn."

Fortunately I always carry a small skein of a strong mercerized cotton knitting yarn in my workbag which I use to hold stitches; knitters know what I mean. Ron produced his Swiss Army knife and cut a couple of good lengths.

"Right, take off what's left of your shoe, and put your foot in here."

My foot fitted neatly into the crown of the cap.

"Wait, I'll go get a second one – these caps fit into each other. Two will protect your foot better."

He was soon back with an identical cap which he put on my foot over the first one. "That works well. Good, let's see now." He began threading the yarn through the holes, wrapping it gladiator-style under and over the whole arrangement, only satisfied when it was tightly secured.

"Right, let's go," he pulled me to my feet. "See if you can walk on that. At least you won't burn your foot on the concrete."

"Yes, I think I can but you'll have to hold onto me. I look like a sort of extinct duck-footed creature with these visors sticking out in front."

"I'm sure people are quite used to the antics of visitors."

We set off, I convinced that half of Volos was staring at me, but there were few people about. "We'd better hurry, Ron, everything's busy closing up."

Ron's emergency solution to the footwear issue worked fairly well. It protected my foot from the hot road surfaces and kept the pebbles out also.

"Well, this isn't Hermes's winged sandal, Ron, but we're making progress."

"Actually, Cathy, this is quite appropriate – you're hobbling into Volos like Jason without his sandal."

"Jason?"

"Yes, Jason. He set off from Volos with his Argonauts to find the Golden Fleece. Remember?"

"I know, but his sandal?"

"Jason lost his sandal in the river right here in Volos … in the Anavros river. He was helping an old woman get across, when his sandal fell off."

"Oh, so now you're calling me an old woman. And look, here's a river." I pointed to a large puddle, a reminder of the previous night's rain. We both laughed. "Yes, I do now vaguely remember. She was a goddess, pretending to be an old woman. She blessed him or helped him later on. Something like that. Those gods were always disguising themselves as mortals, wandering about *incognito*. Quite convenient."

"We'll check out the myth later, but let's try that pharmacy over there right now. See Cathy," he indicated a familiar flashing green cross a few hundred yards away, "can you make it there?"

"Of course. Let's hurry … it's going to close."

The gods must have been laughing down on us from their summer abode in Pelion above, but we did get there, a car even stopping to allow us across the road as we stumbled along. I can't imagine what the driver thought!

Joy of joys, the pharmacy hadn't yet closed and it had a good selection of health-type sandals and clogs in the window. There were two women behind the counter. Both rushed forward as we entered.

"Are you all right, *madame*? Have you hurt your foot?"

"No," I explained. "It's my shoe that's the problem … it's broken. I'd like to buy a pair of your sandals, please."

They both spoke excellent English, so I didn't continue in Greek, figuring Ron would enjoy the conversation. It didn't take long at all to choose a really nice slip-on sandal in red leather, and in my size too. We put the intact shoe and its late lamented partner into the box provided with my new Italian beauties, and went on our very grateful way.

"What a stroke of luck that was, Cathy. Quite amazing."

"Wasn't it, but what did jolly old Jason do, Ron. Do you recall? Did he get another sandal? Should we gather ourselves a bunch of heroes and go have a ship built? Look for a Golden Fleece?"

Much amused, we made our slow way back to the car park.

"Are you sure you're OK to walk in those new shoes? You can wait here and I'll bring the car."

"No problem. I think we should return to Kalamos though. America's waking up now and we'll probably have email to deal with. Shall we eat at Vageli's tonight? What do you think?"

"Sounds a plan ... the food's always delicious. But if you're intending to give these chocolates to Eleftheria ... well, I think the heat might have affected them."

We were passing a florist shop. Tiny, but charmingly set out. "Tell you what, Ron, I'll get her some flowers instead. She loves flowers. She's always got flowers on the tables."

"Good idea. Then you needn't worry about the chocolates having perhaps melted. I can't imagine what we'll do with them now ..." He grinned at me as we stepped inside the floral abundance to be greeted by the man behind the counter. A conversation was struck up, in English for he had spent time in Canada, while he selected blooms and carefully arranged a delightful little bouquet.

"Oh, our friend will love these. She really will. Thank you very much." I took the flowers, Ron carried the rest of our things and we left to collect the car. "I think, Ron, we should check on these chocolates, don't you?" I settled myself in the passenger seat, undid the ribbons on the box, and we set off for Magda's cheerful little house.

HAPPILY BACK IN KALAMOS

No sign of the Bakalonis when we arrived. All was silent but for the sea talking to itself, even the birds having decided to rest.

"We could make ourselves a late lunch, if you like," Ron unlocked our bright blue door, "but if we're going to eat at Vageli's…?"

"No, let's just finish the fruit … it will go bad … and have some tea. I've eaten too much chocolate, that's for sure. We can go across to eat early."

"I'll head to the email tree then. You want to come?"

"No, I'd like to look through this Magnesia book for a bit. Oh, what's this?" I pulled out the thick book Ron had bought.

"That's for you. Look, it's a collection of Cavafy's poetry in parallel translation – on this page is the original Greek and opposite in English."

"There's a lot of work here, Ron, it's not at all easy to translate from one language to another and retain the precise meaning. Not a huge problem in written form – you can take your time to get it right – or in everyday speech, but think of those simultaneous translators, like at the UN. Difficult."

"Meanwhile I'll go see how the ether translates the emails for us. I'm still amazed we can do this. Not like the days of high frequency radio and Morse code."

By the time he returned with the laptop and began downloading the emails, I was thoroughly engrossed in the Magnesia book, and soon Ron was working on his laptop. Somewhere beyond our sight Apollo was being carried in his chariot to bring the light of the sun to others, and gradually taking it away from us.

"Hey, it's getting dark, Ron. We'd better start moving."

Eleftheria and Vageli greeted us with open arms. Eleftheria was thrilled with the flowers, and promptly replaced those already on our table with the bright bouquet. "I know it's a bit big, and I'll take it away when you eat, but for now you must enjoy them with me."

She was the sweetest of women.

"So," Vageli brought our drinks and sat down with us, "What news? What have you been doing? What have you been to see?"

We'd arrived early and there were as yet no other diners, so Vageli could chat for a few minutes. We told him about our visit to Volos.

"You must also go and see the old part though, it's very old, and you can walk there in the ruins. And of course the museum. It's full of the archaic things that have been found."

"Where's this museum?"

"Very close to the hospital. You drive past when you go into Volos."

"Yes, I saw the sign for it," Ron nodded as I explained to him.

Eleftheria came up to the table, carrying a tray with our salad, bread and *skordalia*, that delicious garlic-laden dip which I can devour with practically any food. She had recommended the *pastitsio* for a main course when we arrived: "I'll soon be taking it out of the oven."

I needed no encouragement. If it's pasta, I'm in. Ron – no surprise there – was happy to know that *calamari* was on the menu. Vageli rose to go seat some new arrivals, and Eleftheria took her empty tray back to the kitchen.

"We certainly have a great deal to see, Ron. Should we make a plan?"

"Delphi. Soon. We absolutely must see it."

The food was superb, the *pastitsio* the best I'd ever had. Anywhere. We didn't linger, both of us somewhat whacked after the day's events. Vageli brought us each a piece of marble cake to end our meal which we had no trouble finishing to the last crumb. The taverna was filling up. We went through to say goodnight to Eleftheria in her stifling kitchen, and I grabbed the opportunity to ask her about her *pastitsio*.

"First of all, and most important," she told me, "is not to cook the pasta too long. Cook it for less time than you usually do … remember, it will go on cooking in the oven. Not too long at all, then as it finishes cooking in the oven it absorbs all the flavors of the meat and cheese."

Ah, that struck me as a most excellent point.

"Then after you put the pasta in your oven pan, you must sprinkle it well with *feta*. Mix it in with your fingers. Some people use yoghurt, and some don't add anything. But if you don't do this, it will be very dry and you want your *pastitsio* to be thick and creamy. Your meat sauce you will know how to make …"

One look at my face told her I didn't. At least not like hers.

"Your meat sauce that you usually make. I like to make it with a mixture of beef and pork, and of course your tomatoes and onions. Your seasonings, and garlic, lots of garlic."

She continued preparing salads as she explained to me how to layer the *pastitsio* in the pan. "Make the meat sauce first so it's ready just when the pasta is, or you will be putting the sauce into the oven cold. Then your bechamel sauce …"

Ron heard "bechamel" and glanced at me. I grinned back at him. Yes, I have been known to sieve some of my less than stellar examples, or to beat them into submission. It's amazing what a strong whisk can do!

"But you must have the right spices, that's what can make all the difference. There must be cinnamon and cloves. Food without herbs and spices isn't good – it's like you are eating paper. But yours will be very nice. Make it when you are back in Texas, and think of me."

Quickly wiping her hands on her apron she hugged us both, and thanked me again for the flowers, which she had moved to a small sideboard in the indoor eating area.

"I know you love flowers, Eleftheria, I'm so glad you like these."

"You must come back to us soon. Please. You will be amazed at our wildflowers in the spring.

They are very, very lovely. God sends them to let us know that the winter's over. The flowers make me very happy always … I know the warm days will soon be here again. Come and see us in the spring. You will be very welcome."

Vageli was serving drinks at a table, so we waved goodbye to him and left to walk along the beach. I was prepared, and had worn my hiking shoes lest any skulking scorpion had his sights set on my toes. Back at Magda's we tidied up a little and made ready for an early bed.

The sea lay exhausted, barely breathing, recovering from the hammering inflicted on it by Poseidon the previous night, and murmured the sweetest of songs to us as we slept.

PELION FOR EVERY SEASON

Magda's home proved to be a very good base from which to travel to other parts of Greece, but we didn't feel the need to explore much further afield. The beautiful traditional villages of Mount Pelion and its peninsula were such a delight that we were never bored. Each has its own essence, its history and centuries' old traditions. Each casts its own spell. The increase in tourism in recent years, in particular since the early days of this century and Greece's entry into the Eurozone, has brought about many changes, some for the better, some not so. Isn't it always the case wherever tourist dollars are injected into spots previously off the beaten path? Nevertheless, the character of Pelion endures as it has for centuries beyond counting.

The Peninsula's unique qualities became more evident as we explored it in our rental car. 'Almost an island' is the definition of a peninsula. Mount Pelion's peninsula is an excellent example, extending like a dragon's tail into the water, almost completely surrounded by water. The hook at the very end of this tail is perhaps more reminiscent of a scorpion in the way it curls back towards the mountain's mass. However one thinks to describe it, in imaginative terms or in strictly scientific language, the peninsula protects the Gulf from the worst of the weather to the east.

The peninsula itself isn't big at all. You'll find measurements given of length and width which vary somewhat; these depend really from what points you take your measurement. The mile-high mountain descends in a series of ridges into the sea, a continuation of itself, of its world rich in natural features, but it now adds beaches to its character. Rising rapidly from sea level in the west to its highest point along its spine, the Pelion Peninsula drops rather precipitously into the Aegean Sea on the east.

The mountain has a commanding position overlooking the Pagasitic Gulf. Its highest peaks are still thickly forested and not easily accessible, just as they were in antiquity. Ravines, gorges, valleys, clefts in all kinds of configurations scar the mountain and the hillsides, testament to the turbulent movement of the earth through the aeons and aeons of its creation. Many of these make their way down to the sea, often empty of water in the summer, raging torrents in winter. Some snarl across each other, at points joining into one, speaking of turmoil and frenzy, of the destructive violence of 'quake, volcano, fire and flood which created them. Together with the precipices, cliffs and rock faces they have witnessed both the joys and triumphs of those who lived here in centuries long gone by, as well as their grief and lamentation. They could tell, but prefer to keep their counsel, reluctantly yielding their secrets only when forced to by archaeology or landslide.

Who was here? When? What befell them? Who plied the waters of the Gulf? These and many other questions chased each other through my mind as we explored villages large and small. We came across little clusters of homes hidden in valleys or tucked into hillsides. Maybe these were simply family compounds and not one of the original Pelion villages, but no matter how compact they are and even if they don't have a church, there is at least one *iconostasis* where tribute can be paid to the Trinity and to the saints.

And always I thought of the myths, of the peoples whose imaginations created them, of the bards who brought them to Pelion. I thought of those many generations who respected the mythical gods they held in such awe, believing them to share their human attributes even as they remained invisible and immortal. I thought of how the myths shaped the Ancients' lives, and how we continue to enjoy these thrilling stories in modern life. And I understood why my Mother, an educated woman, held this mythology in such high esteem.

The sea is never far away if you're in Pelion. From the mountain slopes you see it, from the Peninsula you see it. You may be in a spot where you see only the Aegean, or only the Pagasitic Gulf, but there aren't too many places where you can't see it at all. The sea is ever-changing, its color reflecting its mood. It takes its cues from wind and weather, responding to calm conditions by the almost imperceptible movement of its waters. The lightest of breezes may ruffle it a little, waves will chop it up if the wind gains speed, but there's often no telling what might happen if the gods are severely provoked. And sometimes it doesn't take much to annoy them, and most notably Zeus. From out of nowhere a squall can spring up, sharp and sudden, and just as swiftly depart the scene having made its point.

❖ ❖ ❖

Most of the coastal villages have that uniquely Greek seaside character, that familiar and striking setting of white and blue, punctuated by the radiant red geraniums. Traditional rush-seated chairs set out along the waterfront wherever possible invite you to sit, to relax, to enjoy a coffee at the very least. Black chalkboards prominently displaying the menu tempt you to linger. The cheerful servers toil in summer's thick heat, trudging through the sand or darting around traffic while balancing laden trays from the kitchens across the road to tables by the sea. Their energy and patience always amazes me, for it can't be easy dashing from table to table, not to mention dealing with the occasional language difficulties that may arise.

The villages at higher elevation seem less frenzied. Perhaps this is because the popular beaches are so vibrant in summer, packed with sun worshippers and swimmers, with kids rushing about and harried parents lugging all the necessary gear, with people eager to see and be seen. Street vendors entreat one to buy, while peddlers drive through the throngs, touting their wares from vans by means of deafening loudhailers.

"I've got fruit! Fresh, delicious fruit!" they blare.

"Here I am! I'm here with bread, straight from the ovens!" a rival thunders as he cruises along.

"Chairs! Tables! Beautiful plastic chairs and tables!" roars another. "Dirt cheap! Come! Come! You'll find none cheaper!"

Those in the know enjoy the tranquility of the secluded coves that abound on the Peninsula. Many of these lovely spots can be reached only by boat, and great is the delight of those holidaymakers who chance upon an empty beach to call their own. These hidden coves and inlets are jewels of privacy, their location fiercely guarded.

❖ ❖ ❖

Late one afternoon we were driving back to Kalamos from Kottes where we'd taken a leisurely lunch, a seafood lunch we'd lingered over at our table placed almost in the water. Where we'd luxuriated in the peace, the air clear, the sea dreaming of adventures past, and the meal of a quality the gods would have envied. It had been an effort to rouse ourselves when our hostess quietly approached to ask if she could bring us anything more.

"It was all perfect," I told her, "absolutely magical." And it was.

The road was almost empty of vehicles as we drove towards Argalasti. Milina was quieter than usual, Horto seemed still asleep. The Elantra made her steady way up the hill. Nothing else seemed to be moving when suddenly we came upon an elderly woman trudging along the road. Ron slowed down and stopped the car beside her. "She must be exhausted. Ask her if we can give her a lift?"

"Yes, please *kyria*, I'm going to Argalasti."

We got out to help her into the car. She had a basket filled with gardening tools in one hand, and held a large hoe over her shoulder with the other. I glanced at Ron. "How will we get this into the car? We've no roof rack."

"I'll manage. Get her settled and then open your window."

The woman sank into the back seat, her basket on her lap. "Thank you, thank you. You are so kind."

Ron placed the handle of the hoe into the left corner of the back seat. "Cathy, get in and I'll pass this across between the front seats and out through the window. If you could hold tightly onto it, we should be all right."

"I can't imagine what we must look like." I huddled down in the seat with the hoe across my chest and sticking out the window. "What if the police stop us?"

"Have you seen any lately?"

"Well no, but it would be just our luck. Mind you, maybe nothing surprises anyone out here in these parts."

"We've seen far more crazy stuff being balanced on cars and bikes. Anyway, ask her if she's OK."

"I'm fine, thank you, *kyria*. We were working all day on our land to prepare for the olive season."

I told Ron this.

"Who was she working with, Cathy? There's nobody else around."

Up the hill we drove, the hoe in prominent display. "I feel we should have tied a red rag on it, Ron. You know, a warning."

A couple of bends further on a man on a donkey appeared. He was old, somewhat shrunken, sitting sidesaddle on the animal, and twirling worry beads.

"My husband," announced his good wife from the back seat.

"Uh, Ron," we crept past, "that's her husband."

"I know what you're thinking, Cathy, but we don't know what they've worked out between themselves. She's much younger … maybe he's unwell."

"I suppose, but …"

"Things are different in these parts. It's a very rural community – it's not for us to pass judgment. It's not how we live our lives, yes, but it doesn't necessarily mean he's a bad man."

"My husband … he's a very good man. A good man," our passenger said, perhaps understanding the gist of our comments, and we believed her.

She asked if we could drop her just outside Argalasti, which we did. I disentangled myself from the hoe while Ron helped her out.

"I will wait for him here. He won't be long now. I will walk back to the house with him. Thank you very much, you are good people. May God be with you."

She settled herself down at the side of the road and we turned towards Kalamos, to return to the temporary reality of our beachfront life at Magda's.

❖ ❖ ❖

Winter is another story altogether at the beaches. This is very evident in the southern half of the Peninsula, where some areas become quite deserted then. It's the absence of color that emphasizes that it's winter, that summer has taken herself off to another part of the globe. Gone are the bright flowers in their tubs, the brilliant blooms of the climbing plants. The forlorn bougainvillea cling to their balconies, twisted branches stripped bare. There's no beach paraphernalia shouting its vivid colors from roadside kiosks, no neon umbrellas in the sand.

Drab's a good word to describe the street scenes of the wintry southern Pelion. Houses are securely shuttered up, standing stern and silenced. Sheets of plastic are nailed to the doors and windows of buildings which are close to the water, for apart from rain and seawater entering the structures, winter's furious seas hurl rocks, logs and all manner of debris high onto the shore. Visitors to Pelion are often astounded to learn that winter lasts for several months, and although it's generally mild, snow is not all that uncommon.

"No!" you will often hear. "Pelion doesn't have snow. Does it really? How can it have snow?"

One can understand their confusion when all they've experienced here is endless blue sky and blinding sunshine. Imagine the reaction when they learn that Mt. Pelion has a pretty decent ski resort. It does indeed snow, and some winters it may snow a great deal. The east side of the mountain and the peninsula get the worst of it, exposed as they are to vicious winds slicing across from Russia. The Aegean islands of the Sporades with their gorgeous beaches, a summer paradise for all who like to sail upon these waters or dive into its fascinating depths, don't always escape the attentions of Chione, the Greek goddess of snow. Nor does her father, Boreas, god of the north wind, tend to ignore these islands. The Sporades, like Mt. Pelion and the mountain villages of east and upper Pelion, quite frequently receive the undivided attentions of father and daughter, and occasionally much damage is done. The gods are fickle. The Ancients were well aware of that.

TRAILING UP TO TSAGARADA

Ron was making the first cups of tea and coffee of the morning. "Isn't today the equinox? What's the date?"

"Hang on, I'll get my diary." I retrieved it from the bedroom. "Yes, good for you. It is indeed. Should we be doing something special? You know, to welcome the arrival of Autumn, or Fall, as you would say."

"Like what? Have you any ideas?"

"Well, doesn't Persephone go back to Hades now? And Demeter gets very distressed, right? Winter's coming. There's the harvest she needs to attend to. I know, what if we drive up the mountain?"

"Any special reason you want to go to the mountain?"

"Let me get the guidebook … yes, when we were coming back from Argalasti yesterday, I noticed that the leaves are turning on Pelion. There's lots of autumn foliage up there on the mountain now. It must be quite something to see close up. Ah, thanks."

Ron had placed my mug of tea on the table in front of me. "Drink up and I'll make you another. So, have you any particular place in mind?"

"Tsagarada. Here it is in the book … look. It has this huge tree. Can you imagine the view?"

"It will be spectacular, yes, but Cathy, everywhere here has a beautiful view. Okay, we'll go. Let's eat something. Let me get the email and we'll make a day of it."

The Bakalonis were drinking their coffee as we approached later. "*Kalimera, kalimera.* You're out early today. Are you going somewhere special?"

"Yes, we thought we'd drive to Tsagarada. It must be very pleasant there now."

"Oh yes, for sure, and it will be much cooler than down here. The weather will be good today."

"I hope so," I laughed, "not like the other night. That was quite scary."

Kyria Katina shrugged. "The winter is coming. Slowly, but it's coming. The weather changes. We have storms. Some years the winter is very bad."

Bakaloni nodded. "But you will not be here in winter. People want to come on holiday in the summer. They don't want wind and rain."

"Yes, I can understand that. They come for the sun."

"We don't stay here in the winter. It's much better in Argalasti. Cold. But here, on the water, *ochi, ochi*. No, no."

"I hope you have a nice day," I said as we took our leave.

"They look tired, Ron, they work hard through the summer."

There was no sign of her-who-monitored-all-parking. Her property was well secured, so perhaps she'd already closed for winter. Ron drove. I knitted. There was little activity in Argalasti, but it was mid-week and it tended to be somewhat quieter then.

The road was also very quiet, with hardly any traffic on it. Almost overnight, signs of the approaching winter had become evident. Maybe I'd just become more conscious of the changing of the season, or perhaps I simply hadn't noticed, but summer was playing out its last few days. The fields had turned brown. Neatly bound bales of hay awaited collection.

We drove past a lumber yard where workers were cutting wood with vicious-looking machinery. Others were loading sawn logs into tractor-trailer combinations. Sawdust lay about in heaps. There was a sense of urgency though I couldn't think why.

"They're very busy, Ron. In a hurry. That's just when accidents happen."

"They seem to know what they're doing. It's all quite organized. Bakaloni told us the winters are long and I expect a great deal of firewood is needed. They have to be ready. These older houses rely on fireplaces – they'll burn wood for heat. Maybe even for cooking."

"I hadn't noticed all these pine forests, Ron, but just look how much ground they cover. Are they cultivated, do you think? You know, grown as a crop?

"I wondered about that. Somehow I don't think so … I think it's indigenous, just part of the great forests Pelion's famed for. The trees are growing very densely together. I don't know much about forestry, but I'd expect there to be logging trails so they could easily fell the trees and transport them out."

"Maybe they're grown for firewood?"

"No, pine's too soft for that. It burns too quickly. You need hardwoods for heating. It burns long and slow. Maybe pine cones are used, for kindling, but you'd probably burn pinewood if you had nothing else."

We turned off towards Neochori, and began to travel uphill, pine forests stretching away into the distance.

"Neochori means 'new village', Ron. That's interesting – does it mean that a new village was established at some point? As in the people abandoned a former village for some reason? Why would they do that?"

"Many reasons come to mind. Perhaps some form of destruction. Fire maybe, or flood. Or attack. Pelion was often attacked by pirates and brigands, then of course there were the Turks. And also, there was wealth here because of the seafarers, the merchants. Many of them became very rich from trade. Rich pickings for robbers."

I shivered. "How ghastly. I've got to find out more about the history of this area. It's fascinating … I know very little about it. Nothing really."

"We're talking modern history now, Cathy, it's the ancient history of Pelion that interests me, the Bronze Age. And still so much to be discovered."

"Well, we're pretty much in the modern stone age here," I laughed. "Just look." Large clearings along the road were piled high with pallets of cut stone. "The guide book says Neochori is famous for its beautiful slate. Its many quarries … the stone's exported all over the world. Maybe that's why people moved here?"

"Could be, I suppose, though I doubt that was the reason. Transporting stone in former times couldn't have been easy, even over a short distance."

"Maybe it was simply a good spot to live. I keep forgetting how many thousands of years people lived in Pelion…we know they moved about."

"These pallets are brought here and stacked by forklift, ready for loading onto huge haulage trucks. It's like what Magda told us about the olive crop – they brought the olives to the shore to be taken away by boats. This is a depot, a collection point for the quarried stone. It's easy for the trucks to maneuver here and then drive to the shipping docks in Volos. Quite an operation."

❖ ❖ ❖

Up and up we drove. The scenery was spectacular, the villages charming. Traditional houses, large and elegant, stood tall, commanding panoramic views of Volos and the seas far below. These older houses of the rich and influential, the nobility one might say, were constructed in the centuries when Pelion was prosperous, when silk was produced and people acquired wealth, when trade with foreign parts was booming. But with affluence came the inevitable need for protection from those who sought to steal. The opulently furnished homes of the successful had great need of fortification if they were to withstand assault; the building style reflected that. Tower houses provided a strong defence. Their lower levels were of stone, the walls very thick, the heavy doors barred and studded with iron. Any windows at this level were tiny and tightly shuttered, their purpose utilitarian. The upper stories were lined with the numerous small windows characteristic of the Pelion style which, aside from allowing light and airy living space, ensured early warning of approaching attack.

Rich or poor were equally at risk. The poorer villagers might have had fewer valuables, though this is a moot point for all who dwelt here were constantly subject to invasion. Robbery was the least of the horrors that accompanied it. Murder, kidnapping and rape were very real possibilities, along with the destruction of homes, and very often, of the whole village.

The drive was extremely interesting, most pleasant indeed, in all except one respect – the roads. It's not that they were in bad condition. On the contrary, they were mostly well maintained, but often it seemed they were configured to pitch us off the mountainside onto the rocks far below. Very far below. Yes I know it's perhaps not as dangerous as it appears to me, but that doesn't prevent my legs from turning to jelly and my stomach rearranging itself in terror. Suffice it to say I attended studiously to my knitting, eyes cast down, in parts of the breathtaking ride. Doubtless I missed much that was well worth seeing.

The Greek gods were said to spend their summers on Mt. Pelion, and on this day they seemed to be smiling down upon us for the weather was in very gracious mood. I can quite understand why those ancient deities liked it up there. The slopes of the mountain are dressed in brilliant greens during the warmer months, densely clad in soaring trees and an abundance of the vegetation that lies thick among the rocks and climbs out of ravines in search of the sun. The advancing winter paints the hardwoods in every shade of autumn color, as though giving warning as it begins to strip their leaves, while the faithful evergreens stand guard against the vicious winds and snowstorms of the long winter.

A TREE, AND HISTORY

We approached Tsagarada, securely set on the mountainside. Made up of four smaller hamlets, it's the largest of all the Pelion villages with spectacular views to the east where the Aegean furls out its intense indigo and emerald waters to fade into the distant horizon. Other than the occasional island, the next stop is Turkey.

We found a parking spot and spent some time exploring. Tsagarada and its environs are very lovely. Classic mansions, many very old indeed and well cared for, stand self-assured in established gardens bursting with color, together with more modern but equally imposing homes. A strictly enforced building code ensures that new builds comply with the traditional architecture. Some older structures, in varying states of ruin, peer out here and there from behind trees, hugged by flowering plants and not always evident until you come right up to them, so seamlessly does the wood and rock of their construction blend into the untamed vegetation. The effect is not at all unattractive. Dry stone walls of indeterminate age; skillfully wrought iron gates falling into genteel decay, bereft of their supporting structures; miniature fountains; water troughs; ornamental stone work, carved in a time long gone by; badly weathered marble with inscriptions and carvings barely legible; cobblestones. Given the elevation of the little town and its profusion of trees, the air is so fresh as to be almost intoxicating.

I greatly enjoy studying the old structures, to picture who might have lived in them, who might have built them. Rocks are exposed where the whitewash has fallen off some of the roughly finished walls. The rocks themselves don't reveal age, but they show a style, a technique in the way they were used. Even in their destruction these remains of walls tell a story. Infused with a quiet charm, Tsagarada invites one to pause, to reflect perhaps a little on its history.

"I smell something delicious, Ron, and it's coming from over there."

"I think that's the main square. See the tree? Are you hungry?"

"That yoghurt at Magda's was a long time ago. I really could do with a nibble. It's a bit late for coffee and cake, no?"

"I agree. Let's go across and see."

We walked back down to the square where the famed plane tree of Tsagarada, its trunk somewhere in the region of fifteen meters in circumference, has stood guard for well over a thousand years. It gets a great deal of attention. It should. It features in countless travel guides and is the background to many a selfie. What has it seen? What events have unfolded here that we've probably never heard of? I wonder if it knows of other trees its equal in the area? It's not admitting of any but as the Eastern Pelion is covered in dense forests of huge hardwood trees, many of them plane trees, who can say?

This magnificent tree spreads its shade over the large stone-paved plateia. I love trees. I am

in awe of them. I was a small child in South Africa when a neighbor cut down a loquat tree in his garden. I was inconsolable. Bewildered. In vain did my parents try to comfort me. "Why?" I cried and cried. Why indeed? It blocked the sun, it was said. He didn't like the mynah birds which feasted on the fruit, it was said. They made a mess. They were noisy. I have never forgotten this. I saw it as an act of
unspeakable barbarism.

◆ ◆ ◆

On this day, in Tsagarada's very inviting *plateia*, the long-lamented loquat tree was far from my mind. Here one is surrounded by the classic Pelioritic architecture, of which the church and the nearby restaurant are quintessential examples. Not only does this excellent restaurant, the Agnanti, serve superb food but it's in itself a delight, furnished and decorated with traditional artifacts. We were there around noon at the end of the holiday season so we pretty much had the place to ourselves. Tables were set out with plenty of space between them, covered in white cloths that lent an air of quiet gentility to the scene. One was occupied by two older gentlemen playing backgammon, sipping their *tsipouro*. We moved forward, and immediately a man emerged from the restaurant to greet us. He did so in English, correctly assuming we were tourists, and guided us to a table. Yes, I told him, we would take lunch, but first we needed something to drink. "An iced coffee for now, please. We're in no hurry to leave," I assured him.

And indeed we weren't. The cool air, the birdsong, the gentle sighing of the plane tree as its leaves trembled in the faintest of breezes, was so soothing as we sat there absorbing it all that I began to fear I'd fall asleep, dreaming of the centaurs who'd made this mountain their home. Our server brought two menus, detailing for us the house specials, and left while we decided.

"Maybe should invite Dionysus to share our lunch, Cathy, what do you think?"

"Absolutely! Here we are in the heart of the myths, where the gods are still lurking about. He might be offended if we bypass his offerings."

Ron laughed. "You're really into them, aren't you?"

"You should talk, my lad. You know far more about the godly, or maybe I should say the ungodly ones, than I do. Right, so what will you drink? I'm going to have a beer ... don't look so surprised. A Mythos. It's appropriate, no?"

"Oh yes. Myths. And it's a nice, light beer. Are you sure you wouldn't rather have wine?"

"I'll give the beer a try. The name sort of speaks to me. And you, what will you drink?"

"Well, much as I'd like to pay my respects to Dionysus for all he did for wine, I'm still having to drive back down, so no, I'll not have any wine now. Tonight at Magda's I will."

"You can have a sip of my Mythos, then. It's not going to make you drunk and disorderly. I'll order soda water for you."

We studied our menus. "*Taramasalata*, no question. Maybe *tzatsiki*, or would you prefer *skordalia*?"

"Let's have all of them, Cathy … take our time over lunch. No rush. But what will we have for our main dish? Mind you, we could make a jolly good meal of the *mezedes*."

"True, but for me, *spetsofai*. No contest. This area is famous for it."

"Then I'll have this," he pointed at the menu, "rooster in wine sauce. Do they mean chicken do you think, or is it a point to have rooster?"

"Could be interesting. I'll ask Eleftheria about it, she'll know why not just chicken. I'm going over to take a close look at the tree. If the waiter comes back you know what to order. He's bound to speak English and I'm just a few yards away."

A stone column has been built to support one of the massive branches of the venerable tree – the residents of Tsagarada are justifiably proud of their landmark. A low stone wall around it creates seating. I wondered how deep its roots penetrate into the mountain's soil. Who remarked upon it? And how long ago was it taken note of? Did travelers speak to others of it? I sat looking out across the endless view below and reflected on the long, long history of Thessaly, an area settled well in advance of any history ever recorded here.

The great tree under which I mused was already some five hundred years old when the Ottoman Turks finally toppled Constantinople in 1453; it was tall and strong when the advancing Ottomans took Athens in 1458; it was thriving on Mt. Pelion's verdant slopes when Columbus first saw the New World in 1492; and when the English Civil War began to change the country forever, the plane tree continued to shelter those who also took their ease in its shade. By then Christianity had long supplanted the polytheism which had been the religion of Ancient Greece since time not fully known, but the myths continued to be recounted, to be a part of people's knowledge of their history. I like to think that when folk gathered at the tree to meet friends and discuss recent events, the stories of the myths were told to children who were surely as enthralled as I was when first hearing them all those years ago.

Lost in my recollections of the myths, the stories of heroes, thinking about how people had lived and been shaped by the landscape of Pelion, I hadn't noticed that our food had been brought to the table. Ron suddenly appeared in front of me.

"You coming to eat? The food's arrived."

"Sorry, I was worlds away. You know, I can almost believe in the idea of past lives. Like I lived here when the myths were still an important part of people's existence."

"Maybe you did, Cathy, maybe you did."

❖ ❖ ❖

We walked back to our table, which was laden with *meze* and our drinks. Ron poured my beer. I took a sip. "I can see why the idea of centaurs was so strong. There are parts right here where you can't see through the trees, so imagine it thousands of years ago … the dense forests … the centaurs flitting about. If I sit here long enough, Ron, and drink enough of beverages befitting Dionysus, I might begin chatting to centaurs."

"Here, taste this," he handed me a piece of bread spread with *tarama*, "and be sure to talk only to Chiron when he arrives, and not to the others, the baddies."

Our server came over with a plate which he managed to make room for on the table. "This is from us, this is for you from us." In Greek he explained to me what I already knew, that we would not be paying for it. That wonderful Greek generosity which we constantly experienced. *Philoxenia.*

The dish contained pickled anchovies. These are delicious, and are served typically as *meze*, but I can eat them anytime. Each cook has his or her own twist on the pickling process. I understand they're a bit of a fuss to prepare for aside from cleaning the fiddly little fish, they must first be cured in salt. When that process is complete, the next step is vinegar. A very good quality vinegar must be used, I'm told. Some people make their own wine vinegar. "I will not use that stuff from the shop," an older lady explained to me when I'd asked. "I do it like my grandmother did, and she knew it from her grandmothers."

The fish must be rinsed thoroughly before being immersed in olive oil. Plenty of garlic is essential. The pickled anchovies can then be kept in the fridge and served as desired. Our dish contained tiny slivers of onion and red peppers, and was very tasty indeed.

"I wonder how they kept things cool in former times?" I soaked up the oil from my plate with a chunk of the fresh bread. "Although up here it is much cooler than at the coast."

"They'd have had to eat it all as soon as possible, at least in the summer, I would guess. Pickling like this ensured that nothing went to waste."

Greece is no stranger to food shortages; the country has suffered many a famine through the ages. The server arrived with our main dishes, and cleared away most of the *meze*. Ron and I looked at each other. No need to speak. We were both wondering how we'd ever be able to finish it all, but of course we did.

"How's your rooster? This *spetsofai* is something else. Here, pass your plate." I used the serving spoon to put sausage cooked in green peppers, tomatoes and seasonings onto Ron's plate. "No, thanks, I don't want any of your rooster, it might spoil the taste of my food. This sausage is divine … I imagine it's produced locally. I'm trying to figure out the herbs and spices in it."

Our attentive waiter came by to ask if there was anything else we needed. The backgammon players – the game is called *tavli* in Greek – had left, presumably to go home to their wives for lunch.

"Thank you, I don't think we can eat another thing," I assured him, "but it's rather empty here now, isn't it?"

"Don't worry, it is full every night. People come from Volos to enjoy themselves. Many nights we have music. Greek music. *Bouzouki*, clarinet, violin. People dance if they want. And anyway, you have eaten your lunch quite early, others will be here soon. "

"And in winter, do you close in winter?"

"Oh no, we're open all year. Winter is a very busy time. People tell us it's the best time. There are many places to stay here in Tsagarada. People come to spend a few days. We have snow. Some years it's very bad , but we're used to it. For us, it is nothing."

He cleared our table, and then brought the bill, along with two pieces of cake.

"Ron, no way can I eat that now. Not even I, with my sweet tooth, can manage any more food. I wonder if he'll mind giving it to me to take away?"

"You can but ask … I'm sure he won't."

And of course he didn't, and when we opened the foil container later at Magda's, we found a third piece of cake had been added. Very kind. Very thoughtful.

"Is there anything else you want to see or should I get the car?"

"Let's just drive back slowly, but first I'd like to take a few photographs from up here. These houses, they're strongly fortified. Look at the shutters, Ron, they look very solid, but imagine being inside, terrified, with brigands trying to get in. And no communications systems. No phones, no radio. Awful."

"Yes, definitely, but I'm sure there were warning systems of some sort set up. Church bells would surely have rung out warnings. There'd be scouts, lookouts, who'd pass on the alarm. That sort of thing."

"And Ron, the Turks and the pirates were in these parts way before Greece came completely under Ottoman rule. How did they get here from Turkey? Did they sail across the Aegean down to the coast, and then climb up the mountain slopes?"

"I would think so, yes. All kinds of people traveled about these seas. For centuries. Think of Xerxes ... he sailed his fleets down here from Persia on his way to invade Greece. The Greeks tried to cut off the Persians at Thermopylae – you know that story very well. There was the great battle of Salamis. Many others ... there were endless battles in ancient times. The folk here on the mountain, and all over Thessaly, were attacked again and again."

"They must have lived in a state of constant alert. I'm sure they'd have been making offerings to the gods, praying for help. I can't imagine it. Horrible. But I suppose that's more or less every country's history in some form or another. The Greeks had a bad time, but then so did all my Scottish ancestors, what with the Vikings barging about. It's the same today, isn't it? What's changed? There's war somewhere all the time."

"That's how the world is, Cathy. Nothing really changes … just the details. Can you imagine how gorgeous it is up here in winter? Like the waiter described … roaring fires, hearty winter dishes, wine."

"I suppose. But it won't look anything like it does now. And the sun will be keeping a low profile most of the time, so everything will be gray. And cold. And horribly wet. It will be difficult for some people, even today when life is so much easier than it was in the past."

'Well, a 4WD is very useful in winter weather, but they're prepared for it. And there'll be snowplows."

We turned back towards the car. "I'm thinking of the ancients, Ron, how tough it must have been … impossible to imagine how harsh."

"They'd have managed pretty well, I would think. They were accustomed to their life. There were people here since prehistory. They'd have had their fires, and their meat from the hunt. And they'd have sat around, pretty much like we do today, and chatted, told the stories of the gods … of the ancient heroes. It can't have been too terrible … they survived through to modern times."

COMING DOWN THE MOUNTAIN

Tsagarada had made an indelible impression on me. It's ancient and it's modern. All at the same time. Greatly changed, yet unchanging. That particular day it was very quiet so perhaps one could more easily slip into flights of fancy. Had it been packed with people, tour buses belching along, noisily frenzied, my thoughts would doubtless have taken a different direction.

My fingers flew along the knitting as we made our way down the mountain towards the Gulf, my imagination keeping pace as I pictured the ways of life in the Paleolithic, then the Neolithic ages. We've been conditioned to think of these early people as primitive, as unthinking brutes, but they weren't. Archaeology and anthropology have shown, definitively, that this view is incorrect. They were every bit as smart as we, and as capable as we of adapting to their circumstances.

"Ron, do you think the Ancients were actually more intelligent than us? That we today are just building on what earlier peoples discovered?"

"No, they had their challenges and we have ours. I don't see it as a question of intelligence necessarily. They made use of what they had in dealing with issues facing them, what they physically had, or could obtain, and what body of knowledge they had built up. And when they had leisure time, they would explore ideas to see how they could better their lives."

"So you're saying that we're their equal, or they were our equal, in terms of brain power?"

"Absolutely. No question. They had to be … if they didn't adapt, they'd have died. Some groups must have."

"Maybe they died because of conditions beyond their control though … like disease, but it's fascinating, isn't it? They had their engineers – people who worked things out - and they had their artists. I wonder if there're any cave paintings around here? I must try to find out."

Ron drove and I studied the surroundings, the escarpments where caves abound. Many will be completely screened by the vegetation which gives Pelion its character, and some will be forever inaccessible because of landslide. The region is earthquake prone, but seismic activity doesn't always obliterate – it sometimes reveals. And there is much still to be discovered here, as any archeologist will tell you, in spite of all the history that has already been unearthed and documented.

A wind had come up. It made itself known by the swaying of olive trees that grow in orderly rows in timeless groves. The moving air flipped the gray-green olive leaves over in graceful formation, *a corps de ballet* of branches, rippling in a wave of silver as the underside of the leaves was exposed.

"Ron, when did the Greeks begin to cultivate olives? They feature so much in vase paintings and the like. And olive branches being offered, and olive wreaths … you know … ancient."

"At least five thousand years ago – best I can remember. The excavations at Knossos – in Crete - lots of olive jars and stuff found."

"Is my memory failing, or wasn't Athena involved here as well? Didn't she plant an olive on the Acropolis, on a rock?"

"We'll have to go back to Hamilton, but yes, Athena had something to do with it. She gave the Ancients something good."

"That, my dear Ron, was because she was a woman. A powerful woman. Those who created the myths knew a thing or two about the role of women in their society."

"I suppose it won't help if I mention some goddesses who weren't all that wonderful?"

"Yes, you've got it – it won't."

❖ ❖ ❖

We were approaching Argalasti. "We'd better get some milk, Ron, some bread too. Bakaloni might not have any left. Do we need anything else?"

"It won't hurt to get some yoghurt. I'm thinking we ought to go to Delphi soon – yoghurt keeps a long time in the fridge if we're away for a couple of days." Ron pulled up in front of the church. "Do you want me to go in with you? Or shall I go get the stuff?"

"No, come with me. You know I hate trying to sort out the thousands of drachmas."

Shopping accomplished, we turned off the main road on our way down to Kalamos. There it lay, a tiny settlement, serene in its position at the water, with the mountain in silent contemplation.

"Oh goodness!" A small group of sheep suddenly surged across the road to surround the car. "Ron, it's a wonder you didn't hit them."

A man came striding along from the property on our right, accompanied by two sheepdogs who didn't appear fussed. Mind you, the fellow didn't either. "Don't worry," he laughed, "we could have had roast lamb for dinner tonight. Thanks for not hitting them though." He explained that the sheep had followed each other, as sheep do, through a hole in the fence.

We all laughed, and we went on our way while the keeper of the sheep tried to gather them together.

"There was more chance of the sheep hitting us, Cathy. They were never in any danger."

"That's only because you're always alert, but there could have been an accident."

"No harm done. You've to pay attention here though … a rural area. No telling what excitement will come our way."

We reached Magda's without further incident, and soon left for the email tree. I threw bread for the gulls while Ron coaxed the email from the ether. The gulls were in particularly cantankerous mood, lunging at me as I tore pieces from the loaf. "Listen you lot, you'll wish you'd behaved better when I'm gone," but it fell on deaf ears. Maybe I should have admonished them in Greek.

REMEMBERING A SPIDER

Back in Magda's courtyard, the sun starting to bid us farewell, we discussed our delightful visit to Tsagarada.

"I'm so looking forward to the photos, Ron. I want to get them developed as soon as we're back home." No instant digital photos then. No immediate sharing of them around the world. How rapidly we've embraced technology. "Shall we go back inside? It'll be dark soon and for some reason I'm tired, and I wasn't even doing the driving. I'm not hungry, but you might want to pick at what's in the fridge."

"And your cake, Cathy? You're going to bypass that?"

With cake on a plate, and a steaming mug of tea, I sat in the kitchen with Ron, he writing emails and I leafing through the guidebooks.

"Oh look, Ron, there's Asimina up there."

"Who? Where?"

"See, up there in the corner. That spider. I'm going to call her Asimina."

"I'm not sure I follow …"

"When I was a kid, a silvery gray spider appeared one day in our living room. She was quite big. At least to me she was. Anyway, my Mother named her Asimina. *Asími* is the Greek word for silver. I don't know what kind of spider she was. There's lots of spiders in South Africa but I don't think she was dangerous. My Mother wouldn't let her be touched, so Asimina lived her life happily up there. Now and again my Mother would climb up with a feather duster … she'd be teetering on a chair … and clear away a part of the web if it got too big. Our maid, Doris, wasn't exactly thrilled with Asimina, I can tell you. 'Madam,' she would say, 'people will think I do not clean properly. Madam, let me take her away.' But my Mother would never let her."

"Magda's going to dispatch her, Cathy, I'm sure."

"I hope not. I'll try to keep Magda out of here. You're right, Asimina's namesake has no chance against Magda. Dirt, untidiness, uninvited creatures aren't part of her life philosophy."

"More tea?"

"Please. The Greek word for spider is *arachne*. Do you remember Arachne, Ron? Edith Hamilton must mention her?"

"Yes, she does. Go on."

"Well, from what I remember, my Mother told me that Arachne was a very skilled weaver. Famed for her fabulous weaving. I had to ask what weaving was because I only knew knitting. Anyway, she explained it wasn't the same as knitting but it did use yarn. Wool. Seems this Arachne got rather full of herself … had some notions of her superiority. I don't remember it all that well but I think she challenged Athena to a weaving contest …"

"That's right, and first there was some disguising of who Athena was."

"Typical, Ron, typical. Those gods were always up to some sort of mischief. Testing the mortals faith in them, I suppose. So Arachne's competing against Athena – that great goddess Athena – only imagine, but Arachne didn't know it was her. So, long story short … there was some unpleasantness. And Arachne decided to hang herself, but Athena unraveled the rope and saved Arachne just in time. Athena, in her wisdom, saw no point in destroying the talented Arachne, so she turned the rope into a cobweb. So that's where Arachne lived. Forever. Turned into a spider."

"I guess the great lesson here was not to become arrogant. Or maybe compassion for others."

"Compassion?"

"Well, Athena didn't let her die – she changed her into something else."

"I don't think my Mother meant the myths to be teachings. She loved them, knew so much about them. She was telling me the stories for the pleasure of them. And now that I think of it, my Mother of course left out the intended suicide part - I read that much later. I can't remember quite how she managed to bypass the hanging bit, but she must have come up with something. Don't forget I never knew that Bambi's mother had been killed - my mother always managed to drop something during the movie and we'd bend down to look for it. I think now that my Mother, after all she'd gone through in the War … she tried to spare me any distress."

"I can understand why she did, Cathy, she wanted only happiness for you." Ron closed his laptop and began spreading a map out on the table. "I need to do this outside on the big table – this one's a bit small."

"I'll come out with you. It's not fully dark yet. Let me wash my hands and get my knitting."

Two gulls squabbled half-heartedly on a rock in front of the house as I joined Ron at the courtyard table. Lazy little waves were hardly bothering to move. I felt the same way, but the book deadline couldn't be ignored.

"You know," he looked across at me, knitting away on my side of the table, "we're not all that far from Delphi. I'd really like to go there. What do you think?"

"Oh yes, indeed. Fine by me. You drive. I'll knit. How far is it?"

"I'm working that out, but perhaps we should spend the night somewhere … no need to rush. Is there any info in your book?"

I got up to fetch the book. "There are hotels and guest houses in the area," I told him when I'd sat down again. "I'm sure we can find something ... let's take our time there."

No smartphones. No apps. Not at that time. You looked at a travel guide. You worked with a map. You followed the road signs – if they existed – and you set off on your little adventure. And a day later that's exactly what we did.

PILGRIMAGE TO DELPHI

"So Magda's OK about not coming to clean tomorrow?"

We were approaching the cement factory, venting its venomous smoke and tinting the fresh sun-bright morning air a depressing shade of grayish yellow.

"It's no problem, she says. She was quite happy when I called her yesterday."

"Has she been to Delphi?"

"No, she hasn't. She said she'd have loved to see it … I feel a bit bad, Ron. I didn't know … we could have taken her with us."

"How could we have known though, Cathy? I expect such a trip was unthinkable for a woman like her, a rural woman, in those days. She worked pretty much every day of her life."

"Yes, it wouldn't even have been thought of. The distance, the cost, how to get there."

Once we had driven through Volos, we turned off onto the Athens road, passing through an area which seemed to be a major gardening center. Plant nurseries, ablaze with great masses of colorful plants, lined the road on both sides. Stone masons abounded. These offered all manner of outdoor furniture, and an amazing variety of barbecues, traditional ovens and elaborate constructions with spits for roasting whole animals. Arrays of building materials were interspersed among these items so that the buyer could plan the layout that would best suit his needs. I have seen some impressive outdoor cooking setups, with tiled countertops, storage cupboards and built in refrigerators, to rival even the most well-equipped indoor kitchen. Summertime is outdoor time in Greece. Nobody's interested in cooking indoors, heating up the house, missing out on good weather, spending time away from the company.

"Aha! Just what we need, Cathy."

I followed his gaze to a business crammed with marble items, from planters and pavers, to sculptures and statues, from fountains to friezes, plaques and pebbles, benches. Whatever could be carved from marble was on display. "Oh yes, indeed, my lad. That Aphrodite over there, for example, that almost lifesize one … you thinking of her for Austin? Wouldn't she just look terrific in our Texas backyard, among the live oaks, the acorns raining down on her in winter?"

We laughed.

"Seriously though, Ron, some of these little stone fountains are very attractive. If I lived here, I'd want something like that … but copies of classical statues, I think not."

We took our time driving through this one-stop landscaping mecca. Business was brisk, with trucks loading and unloading items, particularly the rock and stone goods. "Why so busy, do you think, Ron? At this time of year are people still adding to their garden plants?"

"It's cooler now, so maybe this is the time to build outdoors. Gazebos and that type of thing. Would be far too hot to do that in summer."

Almost all road signs were only in Greek then, usually written in lower case which I didn't yet read very well, but Ron, a physicist, helped out with the Greek letters and we managed just fine as we drove about Pelion in our dependable little Elantra. We did have some amusing moments though, for we had invariably passed the signboards by the time our combined efforts had deciphered them. Many U-turns were required along the way as a result.

"We should be approaching the turnoff to Delphi soon. Have you seen any signs yet?"

"No, nothing."

"Well, Thermopylae, the monument, is on this road. If we come to it we'll definitely have gone too far.

"Should we stop and look at it then, Ron? You'd have to double back anyway."

"I'd rather not miss the Delphi turnoff. I'd planned to see Thermopylae on the return trip to Athens."

The road was busy, not surprising as it was the main road from the north to the capital city. Ron required all his concentration to negotiate the traffic, which on this day seemed to consist almost entirely of very heavy duty vehicles transporting goods through Europe, Athens presumably being the final destination. I knitted away, checking the road signs and trying to decipher the foreign lettering on all those trans-European monsters. Rumbling along on their many and massive wheels, sometimes in great convoys, these articulated trucks looked like some kind of caterpillars in a sci-fi movie.

❖ ❖ ❖

We reached the turnoff for Delphi without incident and began the circuitous climb up and around Mt. Parnassus. Part of the Pindus range which is sometimes referred to as the backbone of mainland Greece, Parnassus is visible from the Pelion Peninsula. It's about half as high again as Mt. Pelion. We could see its peak from Magda's house, but it isn't the highest mountain in Greece. That distinction belongs to Mt. Olympus which lies in the Olympus mountain range, between the regions of Thessaly and Macedonia. The summit of Olympus can rarely be seen as it's typically shrouded in cloud - a feature most advantageous for the Olympian gods who conducted themselves in unseen and mysterious ways up there.

Delphi is situated against the side of the mountain from where it commands a spectacular view over the Gulf of Corinth. Its location is imposing. The area was inhabited centuries before construction of the religious site was begun in the 8th century BC. One of the most dramatic of ancient Greek archaeological sites, it was of enormous significance to the Greeks of antiquity for whom it was a place of worship, drawing pilgrims from all over the world of its time. The temple of Apollo dominated. Apollo himself was venerated throughout the Greek world, portrayed as a magnificent figure of a man both physically and in his numerous virtues.

Eagles soar high above its crags, riding thermals, swooping down on prey that frequently only their eyes can see. I watched them, wondering if they and their ancestors knew anything about the mythological role of eagles in the founding of what the Ancient Greeks considered to be the navel of the world. Zeus, king of the gods, wasn't all-knowing, but he was very interested in many things. In order to establish the center of the world, he sent two eagles flying towards each other from opposite ends of the earth, and where they met he determined it to be. That area was Delphi.

Parnassus and Delphi had been of great interest to European travelers even before the temple site was excavated, while Greece was still under Ottoman rule. Lord Byron, held by Greeks to be the greatest of all Philhellenes, revered as a hero of the Greek War of Independence from the Turks, visited Delphi and subsequently wrote that he *"Sighed o'er Delphi's long deserted shrine."*

Today Delphi is an UNESCO World Heritage Site, a major tourist attraction, drawing visitors by the coachload to Delphi and its temples in the summer months. The ancients would be astounded by the numbers who come from across the world, a world they had no knowledge of, to walk among their sacred sites, speaking in languages they would not recognize, and for whom the purpose is not to worship but to look, to observe. Scholars study and marvel, adding to their knowledge base, while those less interested mingle, hopefully taking away at least a tiny something of the experience.

The National Park of Parnassus where endangered flora and fauna enjoy sanctuary is also hugely popular. For hikers the area is a paradise. There are numerous caves where significant objects must yet be awaiting discovery; one can only guess at what is still to be learned. For snow sports the slopes of Parnassus are covered with deep snow in winter, making it a major skiing center, popular with Greeks and foreign visitors alike. Those whose lives were centered around the Olympian gods would today be astounded to see the skiers flying down the runs, criss-crossing the terrain in brightly colored ski gear. I leave these activities to those of more sporty bent for, like the ancients, I don't ski, but I share their enthusiasm for the awe-inspiring site which never fails to enthrall and humble me.

The road trip from Magda's took about three and a half hours, much longer than if one were able to travel as the crow flies. Upon arrival we had no difficulty finding a hotel and were soon comfortably settled into the Amalia, from which we set off to inspect the local restaurants in search of a good evening meal. We were not disappointed.

"It's interesting how the menus vary from area to area," I waved the menu at Ron. "Some interesting dishes here."

"So, what looks good?"

"Shall we start with a selection of *meze*? And to drink? You're not driving now, Ron. White wine? Shall I get a half liter?"

The waiter was hovering, eager to help. I asked him for his house wine, and for suggestions as to *mezedes*. He and I settled on *skordalia*, tzatsíki and *saganaki*. "What cheese are you using for the *saganakí*?"

"*Kefalotyri*, *kyria*. Shall I do it with *garides*?"

I nodded.

"I've ordered the fried cheese with shrimp. I think you'll like it, Ron. The cheese they'll use is from sheep milk."

"Sounds good. Are you hungry enough for a main dish?"

"Yes, I think so. I'll decide when we've had some *meze*."

The wine arrived in the familiar half liter jug, together with the bread in a basket lined with a white cloth napkin. Our waiter arranged cutlery at our place settings.

"Rather upmarket, no?" Ron grinned. "Not quite the beachfront taverna."

"And note he hasn't covered this sparkling white tablecloth with a paper one. We'll have to mind our table manners very carefully, my boy. No making a mess of the cloth."

"Getting airs above our station, are we?" Ron poured the wine and we sipped it, taking in the striking view of the valley spread out below.

"Can you imagine what it must have been like getting up here in former times, Ron? In antiquity

… you must have really wanted to make the pilgrimage."

"I'm not sure it was as difficult as you think. Even nowadays donkeys and horses are used in terrain such as this … they can go where vehicles can't. I expect providing the animals to the pilgrims was a good little business. But it was a long trek."

The *meze* arrived.

"It looks wonderful," I told the waiter as I thanked him. "We'll order our main dishes in a bit."

"Today, *kyria*, we have fresh *calamari*, if you would like. Or maybe the gentleman would like a mixed grill."

"Fresh *calamari*? Not frozen?" Ron pricked up his ears.

"Believe it or not, yes, they do have fresh."

The waiter who understood English though he was a little reluctant to speak, nodded. "Yes, our man went fishing today. He has just come back."

"Ron, they have rabbit – you love rabbit. Would you like that instead of *calamari*?"

Ron hesitated. "It's tempting, but no, I'll stick to *calamari*."

The waiter made a note. "And you, *kyria*? What will you have?"

"The *gemista* sound good, but so do the *dolmades*. I don't know which to have."

We discussed the merits of these dishes.

"I can bring you both, *kyria*. I will ask them in the kitchen to give you smaller helpings, if you like."

"An excellent idea! Thank you very much."

"I've ordered stuffed tomatoes and green peppers, Ron, that's called *gemista*. And also *dolmades* – but you know what those are."

"The stuffed vine leaves?"

"Yes. I didn't order any salads though. With these *meze* and all the other stuff we have far too much already."

We did it all justice, leaving not a crumb. Nor did we refuse the dessert, a heavenly chocolate and orange confection, served in a delicate pastry shell.

"I have never tasted anything as good as this. It's divine!"

Our waiter beamed at us. "Our chef, *kyria*, he trained in New York, but he came back here, to Delphi, to his home. Every day he prepares new delicious foods."

Back at the Amalia we settled on our balcony with the laptop and my knitting. Ron had no trouble downloading the email in the same way that he did in Kalamos but without having to climb the cliff to do it. The night air was cooler in Delphi than it was at Kalamos. Though the sea was some considerable distance below, at least a couple of thousand feet down in the south, the lights of vessels on the water were visible. I missed the sound of the water, the gentle rustling of the leaves at Magda's, but I heard an owl screeching as it went about its affairs and delighted in its presence.

"Ron, Amalia … she was a queen of Greece, right?"

"Yes, this hotel must be named for her. She was married to King Otto. From what I recall she was popular to begin with, but then there was some sort of trouble, political, and they were overthrown. So they went off to Germany to live in exile. I'll need to read up on the details. It wasn't all that long after the Greek Revolution, so things would have been pretty unstable."

THE FABLED SITE

During a leisurely breakfast in the hotel's dining room the next morning, and much fortified by caffeine, we planned our day.

"It's about half a mile from here to the temple site. Should take around twenty minutes to walk. Is it OK with you, Cathy, if we start there? Then we could go to the museum when it begins to get hot."

"Sounds a good plan."

We tidied up a little and set off, I knitting all the way. I did get a few surprised looks as we walked through the town, but once we were clear of the shops we were out in the open road, enjoying the uninterrupted views as we walked down towards the complex. Olive groves abound, as they did in antiquity, silvery green acres and acres of trees gliding down the mountain slopes to the sea. How did the pilgrims arriving by sea feel when they saw the formidable heights they'd yet need to traverse? Great must have been their desire to pay their respects to Apollo, or to consult the Oracle. But they must already have known of the difficulties for Delphi was famed far and wide. I'm not a good sailor – my sympathies lay with those who might have endured a rough voyage in order to achieve their goal.

Still knitting, still musing, I arrived at the entrance to the hallowed grounds. The temple of Apollo is the centerpiece of the spiritual site, and is reached by following the Sacred Way leading to it. This narrow pathway is edged with the bases of statues, all that's left of the many sculptures that once lined the route. A few are in museums, but many are missing, most likely destroyed or in private collections somewhere. There was no indication of who or what these statues had depicted. One can speculate as to which gods or goddesses, or which mortal heroes, but as far as I'm aware, there's no definitive record. They were gifts from rulers and prominent figures who might have been more concerned with making a lasting impression upon the faithful who viewed them, than of honoring Apollo. Perhaps I'm a cynic.

It's not a difficult climb, but I was glad of my stout walking shoes and wondered how the two climbers behind us were coping in their slip on sandals. I paused to catch my breath. "So Ron, what's different today? Look at all these stalls selling goodness-knows-what trinkets and souvenirs. Chinese made, no doubt. Nothing changes, does it? I read somewhere that even in antiquity tokens of their pilgrimage, proof of admission as it were, could be purchased by the faithful."

"I expect the funds raised were used in the maintenance of the structures."

"I rather think, Ron, that these are for the maintenance of the seller."

❖ ❖ ❖

We stopped in front of the temple of Apollo, that deeply revered god held in highest esteem through the many, many centuries of polytheistic belief. The sanctuary was cared for by a retinue which numbered priests and stewards among their ranks, and by those attending to the Oracle. She was a high priestess of the temple, and would be of a certain age and background, and irreproachable character.

Once the preliminaries had been completed, which included cleansing rituals and the bestowing of gifts, the person seeking the Oracle's advice would be taken to her. Attired in the robes befitting her position, seated on a three-legged stool placed over a fissure in the rock, she'd make her pronouncements. Fumes emanating from this hole in the ground induced in her a trance, during which the Oracle would speak. It's interesting that she didn't pontificate. Her garbled statements and prophecies were deciphered by a priest, and left open to interpretation by the supplicant who had consulted her, who was then responsible for any actions taken.

The Oracle, known as the Pythia, was under the influence of some sort of hallucinogenic gas. One could say she enjoyed the chemical life. Ancient sources noted that the health of successive Oracles was damaged by the constant inhalation of dangerous substances. Those fumes no longer make their way to the surface, a result of the fissure being sealed off by earthquake. Just as well.

You cannot miss the museum. Literally. It's prominently placed. You could, if so inclined and many are, spend days studying the displays. But if you look at nothing else, if you really look at nothing else, you must not miss the Charioteer of Delphi. He was excavated in the Sanctuary in 1896 and is almost intact. He's considered an exceptional example of the bronze statues cast in the 5th century BC, but the fact that he is neither corroded, nor was he melted down, is incredible in itself.

He's lifesize. Superb in every detail of his body, his features, his clothing. And then there are his eyes. Riveting. Challenging you to take your gaze off him. Made of inlaid white enamel and colored stones, his eyes are so arresting as to be almost unnerving.

The Spanish artist Mariano Fortuny became renowned for his work in textiles and fashion design. He visited the museum of Delphi early in the twentieth century, and was so mesmerized by the fine pleating of the charioteer's tunic that he was inspired to create the Delphos gown. This is perhaps the most famous and enduring of all his many garment designs. The processes Fortuny invented to pleat the silk have remained a closely held secret. The fabric has never been successfully replicated, so should you hanker after one of Fortuny's original Delphos gowns you pretty much have to be as rich as Croesus.

A pilgrimage to Delphi, with all the difficulties of travel involved, was a memorable experience for those who undertook it in ancient days, and it was for me too on my first visit there, but not entirely because of the ruins and the Archaeological Museum.

MY PERSONAL ORACLE

The chambermaid at our hotel, a most courteous lady named Maria, had noticed me knitting and told me as we chatted that her mother was a very dedicated knitter. Would I perhaps like to meet her? Would I? Most definitely! There and then it was arranged that Maria, who lived with her mother nearby, would take us home with her during her lunch hour which she routinely spent taking care of the elderly lady.

I've mentioned that Greeks are renowned for their *philoxenia*, which translates literally to friend of the stranger, or hospitality. Maria managed to purchase a box of delicious cakes before we accompanied her home, where she and her mother were the epitome of *philoxenia*.

Kyria Katerina, Maria's very elderly mother to whom she attended with great devotion, was dignified, gracious and generous. Generous in every way. I peppered her with questions about her life, her knitting and other needle arts, and about the Second World War, the war in which Greece suffered immeasurably. The war in which thousands perished from famine. The war in which the Greeks fought with characteristic courage, as they have done throughout the centuries, and about whom Churchill said in the House of Commons: "The word heroism I am afraid does not render the least of those acts of self-sacrifice of the Greeks, which were the defining factor in the victorious outcome of the common struggle of the nations, during WWII, for the human freedom and dignity. If it were not for the bravery of the Greeks and their courage, the outcome of WWII would be undetermined."

Kyria Katerina was a young girl in that war, enduring horrors and atrocities, misery and anguish, like so many thousands of others, and, like all those who survived, suffering the effects for the rest of their lives. I have said *kyria* Katerina was generous, and she certainly was with her material goods, but it's her generosity of spirit that I will never forget. Not once did she condemn, not once did she criticize, not once did she express contempt. She answered my probing questions, she told some of her dreadful stories, but she did not ever pass judgment. Not once.

We drank coffee, ate the cakes, and talked knitting. And did we talk knitting! *Kyria* Katerina was tiny, her body very frail, but her mind was razor sharp, her turn of phrase delightful. I learnt so much from her, and I don't mean just knitting, though she was a fountain of knowledge. She was working on a sock when we arrived, the second sock to the pink one already completed, the yarn tensioned around her neck in the eastern manner.

I was fascinated by her method of inserting the heel into the sock, what the great knitting teacher Elizabeth Zimmermann would call an 'afterthought', and she took delight in explaining the technique to me, insisting on giving me the sock, in spite of my protestations. The incomparable *kyria* Katerina assured me she would knit a replacement for it.

I've watched Greek, Turkish and Albanian knitters, most of whom employ this method. *Kyria* Katerina learnt to knit stockings as a very small girl, and could recollect no other way of working the heel, saying that's how it was always done in her village.

Knitting was a way of life for *kyria* Katerina who could not begin to guess how many pairs of socks she had knitted. "*Pola! Pola!*" she happily exclaimed. "Many! Many!" were the socks she'd produced for herself, her family and her long-dead husband. A widow of many years, she dressed only in black, and was determined, absolutely determined, that I accept a pair of her own stockings so that I could study the work at my leisure. It was impossible to refuse, and I treasure her gifts.

But socks were not enough for *kyria* Katerina. She loved that I share her name, and wanted me to have something to remember her by, not that I could ever forget her. So the last piece of embroidery she had completed was to be mine, for her eyesight was fading and knitting was not as taxing for her. She pressed a beautiful piece of work in counted thread embroidery upon me which I reluctantly accepted; not to do so would have distressed her. I love the painstaking work, marvel at her patience and wonder at the few, the very few missed stitches, which speak so eloquently of a handworked item. I've had it framed, a poignant reminder of a wise and gentle soul.

Meeting this good lady and her caring daughter was an experience that will stay with me always. The warmth and affection extended to us, complete strangers, remains with us still.

Kyria Katerina, then living in Delphi, is my personal Delphic Oracle for she assured me that whatever was to happen in my life, my knitting would always bring me joy.

A MUSEUM OF A DIFFERENT SORT

A day or so later we set out in search of a bakery, with the intention of buying something for Maria to take back to *kyria* Katerina. Even the most simple of village bakeries will sell a few sweet buns and cookies in addition to the delicious daily breads, but the pastry shops in Greece are in another league altogether. The variety of baked goods and sweetmeats, each more tempting than the next, is such that it's almost impossible not to be enticed. We found a well-appointed patisserie where the goodies we chose were boxed and bedecked with ribbon for *kyria* Katerina. We bought ourselves something too, of course. How could we resist?

In common with places catering to tourists, Delphi has many little shops where one might purchase the type of items that tourists almost compulsively burden themselves with. Those bits and pieces that seem so attractive, so desirable at the time but which often end up being donated to various charities, or pressed upon others. We were walking back to the hotel when dramatically colored woven articles   caught my eye. Hanging outside a store, these were of a quality and design that spoke of classic textiles traditional to certain communities in Greece. I needed no further invitation to enter.

The establishment was an Aladdin's cave, a treasure house of artifacts pertinent to Greek ways of life which have mostly long disappeared, particularly those of the nomadic groups. The shop was filled to the rafters with furniture and furnishings, utensils, dishes, ceramics, tools and textiles. Many of the displays looked as if they'd been brought intact to the shop from the dwellings that originally contained them. Either this was how the homes had been furnished, or someone with an excellent eye had arranged the pieces into attractive settings.

There were several chests, hand carved and handpainted in pleasing colors and design. Some had names and dates meticulously inscribed on them, often with dramatic flourishes and curlicues; a few were more than two hundred years old. These dowry chests, prepared for a daughter from birth, were lovingly filled by the women of the household, the beauty and quantity of the items being a source of great pride. The future bride would leave her family home with all that she would need to equip and decorate the home she would share with her groom.

The owner of these museum pieces approached from behind a curtain and greeted us politely, though tentatively in German, then in French and finally in English: "*Guten Morgen. Bonjour.* Good morning."

"*Kalimera*," I responded to his evident relief. His demeanor was quite diffident at first, though the purple shirt he wore was so loud that it almost shouted at us. He appeared too small for his clothes, which I suppose means the same as saying his clothes were too big for him, but the impression was of a painfully thin man swamped by his cream linen jacket. His blue trousers were pulled in tightly at the waist and were far too long; they puddled over his feet, which were encased in thick black shoes. I wondered later if he was perhaps ill, or maybe recovering from some illness.

We exchanged pleasantries, and I began bombarding him with questions about the objects and their provenance. He was a mine of information, and very eager to share his knowledge, his voice getting stronger and he more animated as we conversed. Everything in his collection was made by hand. Every item was vintage. Each piece was beautiful in its own way, even the most utilitarian of articles. I asked about the dowry chests, and he confirmed that several of the carpets, kilims, bed coverings and garments had been contained in the chests when he acquired them.

I shivered at the thought of finding such a treasure chest myself; I might well have passed out from the sheer thrill of it. Textiles are a passion of mine, and these he had in abundance. Complete outfits from various regions, denoting status within the community as is typical in the structure of such groups, were exhibited about the premises. All the textiles were handcrafted, from the spinning of the yarns used for the sewing, knitting and embroidery of their construction, and to any embellishment applied; buttons and fastenings were of bone, wood, shell, cords and silver. Most of the items were exquisite in their workmanship, and very expensively priced, even the fragments from damaged pieces. Perhaps his clientele was well-heeled tourists, for I doubted that any locals would have been much interested. He did mention later that museum curators called upon him from time to time.

◆ ◆ ◆

I was instantly drawn to the knitted items that form part of the Sarakatsan traditional dress. The origins of this nomadic group, now mostly settled into an urban lifestyle, are the subject of debate among historians. Aren't historians always debating? Nothing quite like academic rivalry! Anyway, it's generally accepted that the Sarakatsani are an ancient people, a purely Greek people. They speak Greek; their language has always been Greek. What's fascinates me is that it has many strands, language parts, of the most ancient forms of Greek, which have not remained intact in the development of modern Greek. As with all cultures, sadly, these language remnants are likely to disappear as the Sarakatsani are absorbed into 21st Century Greek life. But again, as with all languages, surely some words will find their way into the everyday language and enrich it.

The intricate designs which characterize the Sarakatsan heritage date from antiquity and are steeped in meaning and significance. The outfits consist of various garments made from handspun cloth and felted wool, all heavily embellished with complicated embroidery and cording; handmade lace is a delicate feature of the women's undershirts and petticoats.

The knitted pieces are not the main parts of the costumes worn by male and female. These accessories, slippers, socks, stockings, gaiters and a type of half-sleeve are knitted in the round, and are of sheep and goat hair spun on a drop spindle. The coarse yarns are then dyed with plant extracts, almost exclusively with indigo, and are very tightly knitted through the back loop of the stitch. This makes them hardwearing, but must be murder on the knitter's hands. The lower arm coverings, called *manikia* which means sleeves, fit from wrist to elbow, and are worn under the blouse and the heavily embroidered jacket; the gaiters are typically shorter and wider, making them easier to distinguish from the *manikia.*

I either do not recall the merchant's name, or possibly I never learnt it. We spent a fair amount of time talking about his stock, and he commented often that I was well informed. The knitted work was of great interest to me, and he was quite aware of that. I have a sizeable collection of Sarakatsan knitting; no two designs on pieces that I own are alike. Such knitted items are getting more and more difficult to source, and correspondingly more and more costly.

Prices were mentioned. I demurred. We continued our discussion. Prices were again mentioned. I countered. His turn to disagree.

Finally, looking at Ron, the little man said: "Tell him to go somewhere and have a coffee. He is surely bored. Come with me and I'll show you my most special pieces in my apartment upstairs."

You have to love the Continental male! To a man, young or old, they seldom miss an opportunity to flirt, to charm. It's a game of the ages, and I can play it as well as he. And it's a game. We both knew it. It has its rules. I played along. I assured him that while I had no doubt his collection of exceptional pieces rivaled anything I was ever likely to see, and that his discriminating eye was as refined as that of any expert in the field, what he had in the shop was so outstanding that I was more than content with it.

"The thing is," I assured him, "if I were to see your very best treasures – and it's obvious that you have collected for many years – I would be distressed, knowing I could never aspire to such masterpieces."

He had not lost face, and I had not offended. We parted on the most amicable of terms, with me in delighted possession of several stunning items.

Reluctant though we were to leave Delphi with its glorious views and endless groves upon groves of olive trees, some of which had witnessed events of the past few hundred years, we had still had much more to see. A couple of days later we drove back down the twisting road to Kalamos. The Pagasitic Gulf lay in welcome, a strange steel blue color enhanced by the darkening late afternoon sky. The water's surface was crumpled, as though a giant hand had crushed and wrung out a cloth, then thrown it down in one sweeping movement to spread itself out. Perhaps there'd been strong winds while we were away.

We reached the spot we'd taken to parking in so as not to annoy her-of-the-parking-authority, but she wasn't home. Bakaloni's was quiet too, and we saw nobody as we walked back to Magda's house. To our great surprise, for we'd told her not to come, she'd left it immaculate for us, even to the extent of cleaning the muddy shoes we had placed outside the door.

"Oh Ron, the poor dear plodded all the way down here and then back up again while we amused ourselves. She must think we're awful slobs."

"I doubt it. I imagine she was pleased that we didn't track mud all over her floors, and anyway, she must have come down to water her plants."

I had missed the sea at Magda's. Its moods. Its tang. The way it teased at our feet as we walked along the narrow beach between Bakaloni and Magda. Lying in bed at night, I could hear it talking softly to itself and wondered what secrets it debated sharing with me. But it never did.

A CAÏQUE TO TRIKERI

Visiting as many of the Pelion villages as we could, we explored the architecture, the walkways and the numerous ornamental water fountains over the next few days. We noted details of roofs, woodwork, doors, window shutters. We studied churches and village squares. We wondered about the many ruined buildings, long abandoned. Some, neglected, had fallen into disrepair, others had been destroyed in the great earthquakes that leveled large parts of Volos and Thessaly in 1955 and 1957, resulting in loss of life and leaving thousands homeless.

Some of these derelict properties, and often the olive groves belonging to them, will never be claimed or restored. The reasons are many, and all are sad. For some, there are no heirs. Or the heirs may work the land, but have neither interest nor funds to rebuild the stone houses. Many who would have inherited have long since migrated and they, or their descendants, have no desire to involve themselves. Circumstances change. Life moves on.

We tried to identify birds and plants, and debated the structure of rocks. We took photographs. We spoke to the local people who were unfailingly helpful in answering my questions. We enjoyed many a good meal during our wanderings, some of them in the most unassuming little eateries that served us delectable food, and we did not, of course, omit to pronounce upon the local wines. Nor did we neglect Eleftheria and Vageli who always welcomed us with open arms, eager to hear every detail of our explorations.

Seated one morning at the courtyard table, we were discussing how to spend the day.

"Remember what Magda said about that island over there, Ron. Trikeri. She told me the island is called Paleotrikeri – that means Old Trikeri – and that the village way up over there, the one called Trikeri, is much newer than the island."

"What does she mean by newer? Not many places around here are all that new. I guess, in the passage of time, being new is somewhat relative."

"We could ask the Bakalonis about it. We're going to go for a drive anyway, so maybe they can tell us. We need to get there by boat, so how? Anyway, let's ask them."

We did, and over coffee learnt that we'd need to drive a fair way down the Peninsula to a place on the water called Alogoporos.

"You will see a school close to the road. It's on a hill. But first the road will climb up and then you'll see the school. That's where you turn right and the road begins to travel down to the water. You can see the Pagasitikos, and the channel between the Peninsula and the mainland. The school's for the Trikeri children. If you get up to the village then you have gone too far, and you will have to go back. You must remember to turn at the school. You will see the Greek flag."

"And then? What do we do when we get to this Alogoporos place? How will we get to the island?"

"There will be a *caïque* and that will take you."

We finished our coffee, thanked him and walked to the car. The Lady Chairman of the Parking Authority was nowhere to be seen. Ron spread the map out on the steering wheel.

"I don't know, Ron, Bakaloni's directions all sound a bit vague. What do you want to do?"

"Trikeri's here on the map. See, it's up high from the water. We'll just drive along, like he said, and see what we find."

And drive we did. Down through Milina, down past the boatyards, beyond the turnoff to Kottes. We passed goats and sheep and fish farms, and then we drove up and up. The landscape became quite barren. Apart from the expanses of stony ground and the stark rock faces, sheep and goats had pretty much stripped what little vegetation was still clinging to life after the long, dry summer.

"There's some sort of building up there, Ron, with the Greek flag. It must be the school."

"Yes, I see it. There's the turnoff. We'll have to travel quite far down again to reach the water. So here we're now on the last bit of the Peninsula – that hook we see on the map."

Shortly after turning onto the side road, we began the descent. Perhaps the best word to describe the view is "overwhelming." It stopped us in our tracks. Ron pulled off to the side of the empty road, and we stared. We simply stared. I had the strangest sensation of being suspended in space. There seemed to be no limits, no boundaries to the vastness surrounding us. The terrain fell away sharply to the left. There was no barrier, nothing to prevent a vehicle from tumbling, rolling, plunging to the rocks below. The water stretched endlessly to the horizon, the sky into infinity. From that height the almost circular shape of the gulf is evident, with Mt. Pelion directly across the water to the north. Below, to the south, lies the channel between the end of the Peninsula and the mainland. Through this gateway to the Aegean, Jason steered his Argonauts as they departed Iolkos for Colchis and the Golden Fleece, stopping, some say, for provisions at Trikeri island.

❖ ❖ ❖

Ron took care driving down to the coast. We came to a small building in a grassy area where a couple of cars were parked. It was deserted, devoid of any people. We left the Elantra and walked the few yards to the water. Wind and wave had worked well with each other to sculpt a little harbor, and provide a fine sandy beach. A fiberglass boat was moored at a concrete jetty along which several tires were fastened, doing duty as fenders. Oars and nets lay neatly in the boat, ready for use, but no evidence of anyone, no sound but the sea.

"What did Bakaloni mean when he said there'd be a *caïque* here? I don't see how we can get to the island."

"Hang on, Ron, there's a sign over there." A somewhat weathered board was fixed firmly into the sand. I went across to read the handpainted lettering on it. "This must be what he was referring to. It gives two phone numbers and says to call for a boat. Don't you just love it?"

Ron handed me the Nokia. "Can you try it? Let's see what happens."

I punched in the first number given. It was answered almost immediately, and I explained we were hoping for a boat.

"Yes, yes, stay there, please, *kyria*. A *caïque* is coming."

"A boat's on the way, Ron. The chap said to wait here."

Soon we saw movement at the harborfront of the island, and a red-painted *caïque* with a mast set off across the water towards us.

"That must be our ride coming along, Ron."

"Yes. A *caïque*. Listen to the pop! pop! pop! of that diesel engine. One cylinder. Unmistakable."

The engine details of our vessel to Trikeri weren't of great interest to me, I must confess, but I could tell it was a fishing vessel and wondered where we'd sit. Or maybe we'd be standing. "Looks like this will be an experience, Ron."

"Let's hope he is coming to fetch us. Maybe he's going off to fish."

The *caïque* arrived at the jetty.

"You the people who called?" shouted the helmsman, a middle-aged fellow in a tattered sweatshirt, a cigarette clamped in his teeth.

"Yes, please."

That brief exchange was in Greek, of course. He busied himself steadying the boat. He wasn't a man to waste words. Maybe he'd had enough of ferrying people about – he looked tired - but he put out his hand to me and indicated that I should sit on a pile of nets. Ron took up a position next to the mast, which was not equipped with a sail, our skipper swung the *caïque* around, and we were off.

I perched on the nets piled in the stern, clutching my knitting bag, and gazed about. Looking up at the mountain from the water offered an altogether different perspective of the villages, the forests, the olive groves. Of how people had lived in that rugged beauty and abundance, ever fearful of invaders. I thought of pirates, and why it was so risky in the days of old to live near the water, of how entire settlements could have been totally destroyed, their inhabitants killed or enslaved. I thought of the dangers of sailing the unknown seas. I thought of the plucky and resourceful people who had developed a way of life here, who had delighted in their storytelling and had left us such a trove of tales.

"Cathy, I think I'm going to lash myself to the mast. Do a Odysseus. I might succumb to the song of the Sirens otherwise."

"Oh yes? Good luck … any seductive songs will be drowned out by the noise this boat's making, and anyway, those sirens are as elusive as the centaurs."

The water itself was calm, barely a ripple, but I'm not much of a sailor and was well aware of the *caïque's* movement. The engine slowed and we pulled up along the quay at the island. Welcoming hands helped me off while Ron tipped our captain, and hardly had we disembarked than the fisherman pulled away again.

Tables set out on the quayside were most inviting, giving me a chance to catch my breath and have something to drink. "Let's sit down, Ron, and maybe I can chat to someone about what we should go and see."

No problem at all. A most genial man, owner of the establishment as it happened, pulled out chairs for us and soon we were enjoying a very refreshing iced coffee. Our host came over to chat, and asked the usual questions. In English, for he'd heard us talking to each other. We responded at first in English also, but when I told him I could speak Greek he called his wife to join us. We couldn't have had better guides. Natives of the island, both of them were charming and very helpful indeed. He and Ron spoke English to each other, while his wife and I conversed in Greek.

"If you walk up the hill from here," they pointed the way, "you will get to the monastery. That's a very special place to see. There's a lot of history there."

"Thank you, we will, but first can I ask you about the island? Why is it called Old Trikeri? Why is there a new Trikeri?"

"There is a story," he began and his wife nodded, "that the islanders decided to leave this beautiful place and go somewhere safer. The pirates attacked them so often that they could no longer live here. They were forced to leave. Up there," he pointed, "is where they went."

He'd been speaking English, but his wife took up the story in Greek. "Yes, the people prayed to God for help, and took three big candles from the church. When they arrived there, at Alogoporos, they prayed again and lit the first candle. They told God that they would keep moving and settle where the third and last candle had burned to its end. Three candles. That's what they called the place up there on the hill. Trikeri. From the three candles."

I explained to Ron that three candles in Greek is *"tría keriá"*, and that these words easily become "Trikeri".

"Yes, but was this island then already called Trikeri?"

I was puzzled. "I don't know, Ron. I think it must have had some other name. I'll ask."

I did. "So how long ago did all this happen?"

"Ah," our host replied, looking at his wife, "that we do not know, *kyria*. It was so very long ago. Maybe it's just a legend. Like the centaurs on the mountain. But this area is very old, very, very old, so who knows?"

"There's likely to be something in the story though, don't you think? Maybe not exactly as it's now believed, but most legends have some basis in fact."

They both nodded and I translated my comments for Ron.

"Yes, you may be right, Cathy. I wonder if we could find out the island's original name?"

"If the story is true, and not a legend, then it would have happened during the Christian era. The three candles ... perhaps they represented the Holy Trinity? Ron, what do you think?"

"Hard to know without more info on the whole story. The three candles? Yes, much more recent times ... Christianity had already eased the Olympian gods out. But this was inhabited many aeons ago ... the whole area goes back thousands of years."

Our conversation continued until interrupted by the arrival of people in search of lunch; our new friends left to attend to them.

"Why don't we head up to the monastery, Cathy? Would you like to tell them we'll be back later for lunch?"

"*Yassas!* 'Bye. See you later. Save us a table for lunch," I called as we passed the taverna.

❖ ❖ ❖

The pathway led past a few houses, and through olive groves. Dogs barked from behind fences surrounding neatly kept yards. Chickens scratched about in the dust of the track.

"That's free range alright, Ron. There's likely to be fox about, like in Kalamos, so if these aren't cooped up for the night, the foxes will practically be having home delivery."

"It's an island. You can more or less control what comes to it. Nowadays at least. No marauders … I doubt there are any foxes now."

The monastery, solitary and imposing, stood above us.

"Phew, I should have realized this would be some climb, Ron. It's steep … and it's hot. Why stick the monastery up here?"

"You need to be high, elevated, if you're going to scan the area for invaders. I wouldn't be surprised if it's not built on top of some much earlier structure. A temple maybe."

Hot and sweaty, we finally reached the monastery, dedicated to the Virgin Mary, from where the logic of its construction became clear – the view is panoramic. A lookout could see from horizon to horizon. The whole structure is very sturdily built, and certainly would be well able to function as a fortification.

"Look at the doors on these monks' cells – the monks couldn't have been any bigger than me, Ron."

"Well, yes, we know that Greeks were small people. It's fairly recently really that Greeks have grown taller. Better living conditions, more food has led to that, I expect. Alexander himself was hardly great in physical terms – he was about five foot. Average for males at that time."

We wandered around. "Look Ron, isn't that the monastery at Paou across the water there? And just beyond is Kalamos. Ah, yes, this is the monastery we see from Magda's. On top of the island. We look straight at it. Of course this is it. I'll look tonight and see if there are any lights."

We didn't explore long. It was hot. I was tired. I didn't do justice to the monastery on this, my first visit, I'm afraid.

Back at the taverna with cold drinks in hand, an array of *meze* and a platter of fish invitingly in front of us, I perked up considerably. The waterfront was busy. Boats large and small jiggled about. There weren't many people though.

"It's because this is a weekday," explained the owner of the taverna which was providing us with all that fresh deliciousness. "There are more people during the weekend. They come to enjoy our beaches, to relax in our little paradise and to eat at our tavernas. We are not many people living here. We are the only inhabited island in the Pagasitikos. It's not easy to work from here. You see these boats," he swept his arm across at the small ones tied up near us, "people go to Alogoporos in their boat and then take their car if they need to go to Volos or Argalasti. By boat is how we bring back what we need."

We'd noticed the lack of cars on the island. A most welcome change from the insanity on the roadways, we both thought. Apart from your feet, a donkey or a bicycle serves you well in such places.   An ideal spot for those of leisure to enjoy, but hard work for the handful who live there, fishing and tending the olives; not at all practical for the rest of us.

"The monastery," Ron began, "can you tell us something about it?"

"Yes, but it was never a monastery for monks. Monks didn't live in it."

We expressed surprise.

"It was built to protect the people of the island. They could be safe if there was an attack. They could move in and be safe. I think it was built in 1825. Sorry, I will come back soon." He was needed at the taverna and hurried off.

"So Ron, you were right about the monastery and why it was built. Or at least why it came to be used that way."

"The early 19th century was hardly that long ago but it just shows you how much plundering was going on. And don't forget that the Turks were still very much present in Thessaly."

Our host came back and sat down.

"Please don't let us keep you. We don't want to take up your time."

"No, no, *kyria*, it is a pleasure to talk to you. The monastery? Yes, I can tell you more. You may know that here in Greece we had a very bad time after the War."

Ron and I nodded. "The Civil War?"

"Yes, I won't tell you more because you seem to know about it. But here, on this beautiful island of ours, where we're sitting now so peacefully, the government established a prison in 1947, a concentration camp. That's what it was. Political prisoners. First for men, and then only women and children. It was a terrible time. A terrible time on top of the catastrophe of the War and the German Occupation … no, we will not speak of it anymore."

The mood needed lightening. "And the centaurs? What do you think, *kyrie*, about the centaurs?"

"Are these stories not wonderful? Still we tell these myths. Still we talk about them. But today, I don't know … do parents tell their children?"

"My Mother most certainly did. All the myths, all the legends of the great heroes."

"Ah, my wife and I were wondering about you speaking Greek. Your mother? She's Greek?"

I nodded. "She is no longer alive, but her spirit lives in me forever."

He crossed himself. "May God rest her soul."

We paid our bill. Our host waited with us for the *caïque* he'd summoned to arrive. Greetings were exchanged.

"Look after her," he told our ferryman as he guided me with great care into the boat.

I sat on the nets and pondered the lives and fates of those who had made this crossing through the millennia, and what remained of their influence.

Back in Magda's courtyard that evening, Apollo having long since driven the sun's chariot to the other half of the globe, I checked in vain for lights across the water on Trikeri. None appeared. The monastery was resting securely.

DEPARTING WITH A BANG

"Shall we see if we can get one of the fishermen to take us around the Pag in his boat?" suggested Ron a few days later. "It would be nice to see a bit more of the area from the water. I really enjoyed the ride to Trikeri island – it made me eager to see some of the others. "

"Good plan, yes. And such a chap would be a perfect guide. I get the impression most of the folk here have lived in Pelion for generations."

"Have you any idea how we can find someone? What should we pay?"

"I expect Vageli and Eleftheria will know someone with a *caïque*, Ron. We can walk over for coffee and ask them."

"I'll run up to the tree and send these emails off then."

"I like this *caïque* idea. Something we must definitely try to arrange." I rose to take the mugs into the kitchen. "Hang on, and I'll go to the tree with you. I can see better from there what the sea looks like … it doesn't look rough from here."

We walked up the hill, and while Ron took care of communications I wandered among the olive trees. A few clouds were scattered around the mountain. They reminded me of sheep's fleece – mostly white, but with the occasional dirty gray patch. I'd observed that these clouds didn't generally amount to much, that they were just posturing as if to remind the onlooker that they could morph into something resembling a large flock, if they so chose, and produce a weather change.

The sea was thinking hard about how it would pass its day. Little waves had formed. They seemed petulant. Maybe because the slightest of breezes was annoying the water, blowing a bit from the north, blowing just a little from the south. Was something irritating Poseidon, making him peevish?

It didn't take long for me to get distracted. Two tightly packed trails of ants were coming and going in very determined manner, apparently to some food source judging by the particles clutched in their mandibles. Aesop came immediately to mind – the age-old tale of the busy, busy ant preparing his winter pantry, and the grasshopper, a cicada in the original version, making music all through the summer days. Maybe the cicada had a point!

The ascending ants were returning to their nest with the food, so the edibles would be on the downhill run. I followed the ants towards the water and saw a dead seagull, the object of their attentions. They were swarming all over the bedraggled carcass. Had it been dead for some time? I moved closer to investigate. I vaguely remember my foot slipping, a split second of panic, and not much else after that.

"Cathy! Cathy! Wake up! Cathy, wake up!"

I opened my eyes to find an agitated Ron crouched next to me. Why was he doing that? Why was I lying on the ground? Staring up at the sky? Dimly registering that Ron was very anxious

I tried to figure out what was going on. Perhaps I'd angered the gods? Had a centaur run into me? Whatever had happened the pain in my head and the spots dancing in front of my eyes were real enough. Turns out one of the myriads of tiny stones and bits of marble underfoot had caused me to measure my length on the unyielding slabs of rock.

We're not sure how long I was oblivious to the interesting world around us, but Ron was of the opinion that several minutes had passed until he came to look for me. He was convinced that I was probably concussed, but no harm came of the fall. Nothing was broken. A few bruises and scrapes. A little nauseous. A bit of a headache. Ron guided me back to Magda's and the restorative qualities of hot, strong tea. I didn't argue when he insisted that we remain quietly at Magda's for the rest of the day.

"Cathy, no, no way are we going to see if we can go out on a boat today. It's not happening. Get some rest and maybe we'll walk over to Galini's later."

We didn't go out again as it happened, opting rather to nibble on what we had in the house. I worked on my knitting, wrote up my notes, and took it very easy. A softly swishing sea accompanied our peaceful sleep, and apart from a few aches I was perfectly fine the following morning.

"It's a really nice day, Ron, it will be fabulous on the water. Let's get moving and see if Vageli or the Bakalonis can rustle us up a boatman."

"No Cathy, sorry, but no. I'm not happy about that bang to your head. I thought about it during the night. You never know what might happen. You were out of it … completely out of it. What if there's some kind of delayed reaction? We'll go back to Athens a few days early, just to be sure. There's medical help there if you need it."

I did see his point. "Today? We're going back today? It's not what we'd planned."

"No, we'll drive back tomorrow. We'll get straightened out here today, say goodbye to people – they know we were leaving soon anyway. It won't be a surprise. We can eat at Galini's tonight, and go in the morning when we're ready."

Ron was right. There was no point in tarrying. We polished off our tea and coffee, tidied up the breakfast things and while Ron walked to the email tree, I began gathering up my knitting projects, keeping handy what I'd work on during the next couple of days. Ron returned with the downloaded emails which we dealt with over more caffeine, writing emails, and contacting the family.

"I'll go up and send these now. When I come back we can make sure that we've collected all our stuff, and are leaving the house in good order. We can pack the bags later."

"I'll have to call Magda and explain to her. I may as well come up with you now and do it after you get the email."

We climbed up the path for what would be the last time for me. I didn't want to go up to the email tree again. I wanted to remember the view of the sea and the mountain as it was at that moment. Mt. Pelion was lost in thought. The Pagasitic was contemplating the day ahead. A *caïque* was moving across in front of me, its familiar sound in strangely soothing counterpoint to the racket of the gulls fussing around it. I wished them all well, thankful for the memories they had provided.

"Right, finished. I'll call Magda for you and you can talk to her. Thank goodness we could get this signal up here – we'd have found it difficult with no phone." Ron punched in the numbers and then handed me the phone.

Magda answered almost immediately. She fussed, as I knew she would. She was upset that we were leaving, was concerned that we weren't happy with her house and her attentions. I stood there, watching the *caïque* disappear around the next headland. I didn't know who was on board it. Who the fisherman was. Whether he was successful. Whether his life was a happy one. Our communications had been no more than a friendly wave each time I'd seen him.

"*Ochi,* Magda. No, no. Of course not. There's no problem." I tried to concentrate on her protestations. "We have no complaints at all. But we do have to go back now." I didn't tell her that I'd banged my head for I knew she'd be very concerned.

"God go with you. *Kaló taxídi* – good journey. Please come back. I love you. I will miss you."

We would miss her too.

"Right, that's done. I'll check in with email again later this afternoon, if there's anything you want to send. So, what can I do here?"

"Nothing, thanks … we've made no mess. Everything's more or less in order. We'll strip the beds for her tomorrow."

"Cathy, look," Ron pointed up at Asimina in her corner, "do you want me to try and take her outside? I can stand on this chair and see if I can catch her."

"No, there's no point, Ron, honestly there isn't. You might hurt yourself … no, Asimina will escape, or Magda will get her. That's how it goes. You know that. Let's sit outside for a while. I want to watch the sea. Maybe the dolphins will pass by again."

"I'll go check the car over then. See if the tires are OK. I'll be back soon."

The seagulls were bickering in their usual bad-tempered way, dive bombing each other in the water, squawking at one perched on a rowing boat. I fetched the last of the bread from the kitchen, knowing that all hell would break loose when I'd toss it to them. And it did. "Ungrateful wretches," I yelled, "you don't know how good you've got it."

"Who you shouting at?" Ron laughed. "I've just seen the Bakalonis. They say come for coffee. At least that's what I think they said. You know …'*kafe, kafe*', so I nodded and said yes. We'll go over later and we can say goodbye."

The Bakalonis wished us well, and expressed the hope that we'd return. *Kyria* Katina told me she was looking forward to seeing my book, and for that reason alone, she said, I'd have to come back and show it to her.

Back at Magda's, we puttered about. There wasn't much to do. We took a long nap that afternoon and when we awoke, Ron walked to the email tree for the last time. I thought it wise to stay at sea level and observe the gulls.

"Let's go over to Galini's in about an hour, Cathy. I've a few replies to write up first, then I'll send them off from Athens tomorrow."

Vageli spotted us as we turned into the courtyard. "Welcome! Welcome! Come. Sit." He guided us to our favorite table – the one at the side next to the tubs of ferns and gardenias that Eleftheria tended with great care. The TV was on as usual, inside the building, its commentary competing with the Greek music from the speakers dangling up on the wall outside. "It's been a very good day. God has blessed us with such fine weather. Are you well?"

We exchanged pleasantries. Then I told him. "Vageli, we will leave tomorrow. This will be our last night here with you."

"Are you joking with me? So soon? But you were here for still more days."

I shook my head. "No, we need to go now. Tomorrow."

"Eleftheria will be upset. She wanted to make you a special dinner when you would leave."

He went inside and I could see him in conversation with her.

She came out to our table, wiping her hands. "I will really miss you. We want you back. As soon as possible. Will you come next year?"

"We'll do our best to come again one day, but I can't promise anything."

Vageli arrived with the customary paper tablecloth which he clipped over the red checked fabric one. I kept my eyes fixed on the items displayed here and there, in particular an *amphora* which Vageli had told me previously was given to him by someone who'd found it while diving. Its condition spoke of time spent deep underwater. I wondered about its age. I still do.

Ron ordered wine and Vageli, continuing to lament our imminent departure, went off to fetch it.

"Ron, that *amphora*, it's very old, wouldn't you say?"

"So hard to tell. It's not of any recent manufacture. I think it takes a while for molluscs to stick to it like that. They're deeply embedded, and those holes bored into the clay … it's been in the sea a long time."

"I wonder if the diver found only this one? You'd think he'd have kept it for himself."

"Well, first off we don't know where it was found. Could've been washed up from just about anywhere. Could have come from an ancient wreck somewhere around. Could have been stuck in rocks near the shore."

"The Pag must surely be thick with wrecks, Ron, but diving's not allowed. Not with tanks.

Only snorkels. And you have to declare anything found to the authorities."

"I wonder if folk always do that, though. As for diving with tanks, who's going to see someone diving at night, with a light? In all these little inlets and hidden spots? And we know that much has been looted. Even in recent times. During the War ..."

Vageli brought the wine and a jug of water. He took out his order pad and pencil. "Eleftheria says she's preparing stuffed *calamari* for Ron, but it will take a little while."

"She spoils you my lad! And me, Vageli, what should I have?"

"I have fresh *bakaliáros*. Caught this morning. I can grill it for you."

"Yes, please, Vageli. Ron, I'm having grilled hake and you're getting your favorite."

"I'll bring *meze* and salads soon," and off Vageli went to place our order.

We continued our conversation.

"The thing is, Cathy, we know it's almost impossible to tell the age of that *amphora*. The shapes barely changed over thousands of years. That's why it's of the utmost importance that artefacts aren't removed from the point of discovery. How they're found, where they're found, what else is found in the area – that's what dates them."

"Yes, I know it's hard to tell with any degree of accuracy if stuff's not in context. Well, I'm going to imagine that it sank in antiquity, in a boat full

of wine or maybe oil jars. There was a storm …
the poor sailors ... trying to deliver the goods … "

Ron poured the wine. "Here's to your wonderful
imagination and any poor sailors who may have
gone down with this *amphora*."

We ate. We lingered over each dish. Eleftheria
produced a magnificence of *calamari* for Ron,
and hake grilled to perfection for me. Served on
a platter with lemon wedges from her own trees,
and a simple lettuce salad, my fish was worthy of
any of the finest restaurants. The magic in
Eleftheria's workworn fingers came not only from
her skill, not just from the knowledge passed on
by generations of her family's womenfolk, but
from the passion she had in the preparation of
foodstuffs.

We hastened back to Magda's, not wanting to
linger on our walk, overcome by Eleftheria's
blessings, Vageli's gruff exhortations to return
and the warmth of their embrace.

Birdsong awakened us the next morning. The
sea had begun to ripple. Little waves were
forming. "Look Ron, Poseidon's agitated that
we're leaving."

"Just as well we are then, so let's get going in
case he decides to cut up rough."

After a small breakfast and not too much
caffeine, we began packing the Elantra. She, the
chairman and sole member of the Parking
Committee was, thankfully, nowhere to be seen.
With a final glance around Magda's house and a
small something left for her on the kitchen table,
we stepped out the blue door for the last time.

Ron locked it and hid the key. We walked to the car. He started it. I took out my knitting. We drove across the river, along the deserted beach and turning our backs on the Pag, began to make our way up the hill.

DRIVING LESSONS

"We'll be passing Thermopylae in a bit, Cathy. I'll stop and we can have a quick look around."

We chatted about the historic events at Thermopylae. My Mother had told me of the battle with the Persians when I was a child, and I was thrilled to see the place she'd described so vividly and with such pride.

The national road bypasses the monument to Leonidas now, although you can turn off the road to get to it. Until the construction of the new road, you would drive straight past the spot, or park in an area from where you would cross the highway to study it more closely. Ron pulled off the road alongside some tourist coaches, and we surveyed the surroundings. He pointed to where Leonidas and his vastly outnumbered men would probably have taken up position in a desperate attempt to block the advance of Xerxes's army. It was an emotional moment for me.

"I think I'll just sit in the car and knit," I said as he prepared to walk down to the highway. "No, no, I'm fine," I added as he gave me a searching look, but fortunately he didn't disagree and went off. I wanted the time with my memories. I could hear my Mother's voice as she recounted the story of the determined Greeks, fighting fiercely and fearlessly to the death to protect their homeland. I was too young then to know of the German Occupation of Greece during the Second World War, and completely ignorant for many years of my Mother's courage and suffering during that horrendous time.

I could see Ron about a hundred yards away, taking photographs, pointing that annoying compass up at the mountain, making notes of the location. His interest in Greek history was sparked in early childhood.

Absorbed in my thoughts, I became dimly aware that one of the coaches appeared to be reversing.

"How odd," I thought, glancing down at my knitting. "it seems as if I'm moving, but it's some kind of illusion." I've never studied physics, but suddenly it dawned upon me that the coach was stationary and that I was the moving party, gaining speed as the Elantra rolled closer and closer to the busy highway.

With a reaction time faster than I'm normally capable of, I managed to move my leg over to the pedals and jam my foot onto the brake, bringing the car to a halt just as it was about to enter the road. Ron came rushing across to grab the steering wheel and take control, while I stood awkwardly between the seats, tangled in knitting. My left leg was doing its best to push the brake pedal through the floorboards.

Ron was profuse in his apologies, explaining that because he'd left the air conditioning on for my comfort, he couldn't put the car in gear, and hadn't applied the emergency brake sufficiently. We were both shaken, and I tease him to this day about how he'd tried to kill me.

♦ ♦ ♦

Vehicles whizzed past as we continued towards Athens, even though Ron was traveling at the speed limit. Drivers need to be very alert in Greece, as of course they must everywhere, but Greek drivers do tend to take some mind-boggling chances. Defensive driving seems not to be a top priority. We found ourselves behind a dilapidated Lada being driven by a very old man, anxiously peering over the steering wheel. His driving was not only dangerously slow on a busy highway, but so erratic that we held our breath each time we and he were overtaken by a furiously impatient motorist.

"I've got to get past him, Cathy. There's going to be an awful accident if I don't."

Today that stretch of the highway is bypassed by a series of new tunnels, all part of the massive upgrades the Greek government has implemented, but fatal crashes were quite common. That section of the road was notorious for them.

There was a break in the stream of cars overtaking us, so Ron signaled and pulled out to pass the Lada. At that precise moment the old boy swung to his left, causing Ron to straddle the white line just as we rounded a corner into the welcoming arms of a traffic policeman.

Leaning against his motorcycle, clad in black with dark glasses hiding most of his face, he took a step forward and held up his hand in that unmistakable gesture: STOP! Ron pulled over into the wide layby, completely off the road and conveniently located at a perfect spot to trap the unwary motorist, and waited for him to walk up to the car.

First Mr Traffic Officer studied the license plate, making a note of the number and looking comically like a cop in a movie. I expected him to lick a pencil but he had a ballpoint pen. I had an almost uncontrollable urge to laugh.

"Leave it to me," I muttered as Ron began taking his papers out of the glove box, "and keep quiet."

He came up to Ron's window and addressed him in Greek.

"Sorry, officer, he's a foreigner and doesn't speak Greek," I chirped.

He stared at Ron for what seemed several minutes. Ron already had his Texas driver's license, International Driver's License and the car's papers in his hand.

"This is a rental car," the representative of the law stated, as though this somehow compounded the situation. "What are you doing here?"

This was not the time to state the obvious. It seemed inappropriate to point out that as the car was hired, that the driver had an international license and didn't speak Greek, it might be logical to assume we were tourists. We hardly looked like illegals.

My wits, which are in the annoying habit of deserting me rather often, stayed put this time and I went into full Oscar-winning mode. I answered him in deliberately halting Greek, hoping that my utterances would gain us some sympathy.

"We have come for a holiday, to see more of the country, and now we are going back home," I stumbled.

"Where is home?"

"Texas."

His gaze seemed fixed on Ron, though it was hard to tell because of the dark glasses. "Texas? He's from Texas?"

"Yes, he is, we live there."

"You? Are you also from Texas?"

"I live there now, yes."

Mr Voice-of-Authority pondered this bit of information for a while.

"Are you an American also?"

I could have answered in the affirmative as I have long had citizenship, but I made a swift decision not to.

"No, officer, I am a Scot."

"Ah, from Britain then. But you speak Greek?"

I nodded. "Yes, I try. I love Greece."

He thought a while. "Why are you married to an American?"

I shrugged.

He considered this for several tense minutes.

"Tell him," he jerked his head at Ron, "tell him he's not in Texas now. He can't drive here like a cowboy."

I translated for Ron, being very careful not to add any comment for fear Mr Officer-of-the-Law might understand, and making sure to refer to him as 'this gentleman'.

"You do know," pronounced the forbidding figure "that you will have to pay a big fine for this?"

He used, of course, the Greek word for fine, which is *próstimo.*

I did my best to appear confused. "*Sygnomi kyrie*, sorry sir. I don't understand what that is."

I kept my eyes firmly on the black glasses.

"You have broken the law. For this you will have to pay."

I nodded again. "Yes, of course, officer. We understand."

"It will be a big fine. You must pay it. You cannot leave without paying it."

"Yes officer, certainly, but where will we pay it? Can we pay at the airport? We are about to fly back home."

"No, you cannot pay at the airport. They do not deal with traffic fines there. You will pay me. You will give me the money, and that's all you need to do."

He named an amount in drachma which Ron later told me was in the region of $500.

"You will give that to me now, and then you can go."

Ron, having heard "drachma", began to catch on, and pulled out his wallet. "Please tell him I'm very sorry."

I went into full groveling mode. "Officer, my husband's very sorry. Very sorry indeed. We both are very sorry that we've caused you so much trouble. You have a difficult job to do, and we have added to your problems."

I didn't dare catch Ron's eye, fearing that my suitably contrite expression would collapse into a fit of giggles. Meanwhile car after car hurtled past us, most with at least two wheels over the white line, and some with all four.

The policeman stood in silence for several seconds, pursing his lips. I couldn't see his eyes so could only guess at his expression.

"All right," he said finally, "I'm going to let you go. I'm going to let you go because I can see that you love Greece. I can see that you try to learn our language. I'm going to let you go because we are very good people here in Greece. I'm going to let you go so that you remember this. This is a lesson for you."

"Officer, thank you, thank you very much, you are very kind, very kind," I burbled.

"But tell him," he pointed his pen at Ron, "tell him that he must be very careful. Tell him there are rules for the road. Tell him he's not in Texas now. Tell him that he should drive like a Greek."

We drove slowly away, like reprimanded children not wanting to draw further attention to themselves. Drive like a Greek? Hilarious thought!

The remainder of the drive back to Athens was without incident. We arrived late in the homeward rush of the afternoon. The traffic, the noise, the madness of activity unnerved me after the tranquility of Pelion. I missed the sea. I would have welcomed the screeching, the outrage of the gulls, for although they were constantly combative, unrestrained in their behavior, theirs is one adapted to survival. The brain-numbing cacophony of car horns, of squealing brakes, of yelled greetings and bellowed insults that defines crowded cities can also be described as one of survival, but is it one which we have absolutely no control over? In the city of Socrates, Plato, Aristotle I pushed these questions out of my mind as we settled into our hotel, and turned my thoughts to how we might spend the next two days in Athens.

❖ ❖ ❖

"So, what do you think Nikos and Taki will have to say when we give them back their car?"

We were battling the traffic on our return to the airport. "Well, they can't complain about its condition, Ron, we've not put a mark on it. I just hope Nikos doesn't start a conversation about Dallas."

Ron dodged a taxi that had suddenly pulled out from the curb. "Don't worry, we'll tell them we have to hurry across and check in for the flight."

It so happened that only Taki was in the office. He greeted us pleasantly but, as on the first occasion of our meeting, made little comment and quickly completed the formalities.

"Please give our best wishes to Nikos," I said as we left to trundle our bags to the departure hall where, in sharp contrast to our arrival, all proceeded smoothly.

The Acropolis, symbol of Greek democracy and Western civilization, stood in silence as we flew over her, but the whispered voices of the past reached my ears.

THE END

ACKNOWLEDGEMENTS

This book would never have been finished were it not for the support and encouragement that my dear friends Moira Ambler and Dawn Cusick unfailingly gave me. I am extremely grateful to them and my family. Without my husband, Ron, it could not have been written at all, for he made it possible by giving unflinchingly of his time and energy in every way.

ABOUT THE AUTHOR

Catherine Ham

Cathy Ham was born in Scotland and grew up in South Africa, where she became a high school language teacher. She enjoys hiking, birdwatching and travel, and is particularly interested in archaeology and ethnic folk arts. Cathy is owned by a great many cats, all rescues, who enjoy a comfortable, happy life together with a cat-loving dog.

Never without her knitting, which has led to her writing several books on the subject, she has also written a series of science books for children. Although Cathy maintains that she has a poor sense of direction, she can pinpoint the location of chocolate supplies with unerring accuracy. She and her Texan husband divide their time between Austin and Pelion.

Printed in Great Britain
by Amazon